BIG BOOK OF KINDERGARTEN PUZZLES #2

Gospel Light

How to Make Clean Copies from This Book

You may make copies of portions of this book with a clean conscience if

- you (or someone in your organization) are the original purchaser;
- you are using the copies you make for a noncommercial purpose (such as teaching or promoting your ministry) within your church or organization;
- you follow the instructions provided in this book.

However, it is ILLEGAL for you to make copies if

- you are using the material to promote, advertise or sell a product or service other than for ministry fund-raising;
- you are using the material in or on a product for sale; or
- you or your organization are not the original purchaser of this book.

By following these guidelines you help us keep our products affordable.

Thank you,
Gospel Light

Editorial Staff

Publisher, William T. Greig

Senior Consulting Publisher, Dr. Elmer L. Towns

Publisher, Children's Curriculum and Resources, Lynnette Pennings, M.A.

Publisher, Research, Planning and Development, Billie Baptiste

Senior Consulting Editor, Wesley Haystead, M.S.Ed.

Senior Editor, Biblical and Theological Issues, Bayard Taylor, M.Div.

Senior Editor, Sheryl Haystead

Writer and Editor, Mandy Abbas

Contributing Editors, Debbie Barber, Amy Bond, Mary Gross, Linda Mattia, Mary Mleziva, Patti Pape, Becky Phillips, Kelly Thulin, Benjamin Unseth

Illustrator, Chizuko Yasuda

Designer, Zelle Olson

Contents

How to Use This Book

Welcome to *The Big Book of Kindergarten Puzzles #2,* a learning adventure to challenge the kindergartner in your home or classroom. Your kindergartner will be excited to review Bible stories and verses through completing mazes, dot-to-dots, What's Different? picture puzzles, matching and counting activities, hidden pictures and a variety of other enticing puzzles.

The 104 Bible puzzles contained in this book teach Bible stories, verses and values in an age-appropriate way for a kindergarten learner. The puzzles highlight 52 Bible verses, with two puzzles focusing on each verse. One puzzle reinforces the verse through a Bible story. The second puzzle presents a modern-day life application of the verse. Both types of puzzles will engage your kindergartner and provide a springboard for Bible learning.

How to Use This Book in Your Classroom

Use this book as a fun way to review Bible stories and verses and to practice academic kindergarten skills. These puzzles can also provide "something more" for kindergartners who are grouped with preschoolers.

Follow these easy steps for successful use of the puzzles.

1. Before class:

- Find the puzzle(s) that matches your lesson's Bible story or verse: use the table of contents or one of the indexes.
- Photocopy the puzzle(s) you have selected. Make one copy of the selected puzzles for each child, plus a few extras for visitors or for children who want to start over. Leave the back of each paper blank for children to use for each puzzle's Bonus Idea.
- Check the puzzle's directions and Bonus Idea for any extra materials you will need. In addition to pencils, some puzzles may require crayons or colored pencils, scissors and/or glue sticks.

Note:

If you are using this book along with Gospel Light's *Little KidsTime My God and Me* course, the appropriate puzzles (two per lesson) are designated on the last page of each lesson in the teacher's guide.

2. In class:

- Distribute a pencil and puzzle to each child. Read the puzzle directions aloud.
- Assist children as needed to complete the puzzle. Be ready to explain the Bonus Idea to children as they finish the main puzzle activity.
- Talk with children during and after their puzzle work. Your conversation can tie the children's work to the Bible story and verse presented in each puzzle. The printed copy on each puzzle will help you communicate the important link between a Bible story and verse and the everyday lives of your children.

How to Use This Book in Your Home

Use this book with your kindergartner as a tool through which to talk about Bible stories, verses and values with your child, and to reinforce academic kindergarten skills.

Follow these steps for valuable learning and together time.

1. **Gather the materials needed for the puzzles.**

   - For most puzzles, nothing more than a pencil is necessary. Crayons or colored pencils, scissors and/or a glue stick are needed for a few puzzles.
   - You may want to buy your child a set of colored pencils to use in completing and coloring each puzzle.

The Bonus Idea at the bottom of each puzzle often involves a drawing activity. Suggest your child complete Bonus Idea activities on the back of each puzzle, or provide extra paper for this.

2. **Keep *The Big Book of Kindergarten Puzzles #2* in a special place.**

   - Get out the book and invite your child to work on several puzzles a week or, if your child is an avid puzzler, a pair of puzzles each day. (Pairs of puzzles can be recognized because every two puzzles teach the same Bible verse and life-application idea.)
   - Even if your child wants to hurry through the book, encourage your child to complete only one or two pages at a time, so you can take time to review the Bible verse and Bible story presented in the puzzles.

3. **Review the puzzles together to increase understanding.**

   - Sit with your child to find and read the puzzle's Bible verse in your child's Bible. Allow your child to highlight the verse in his or her Bible.
   - Read the verse again at bedtime as reinforcement.
   - Briefly talk with your child about the life-application ideas presented in the puzzles and about the responses appropriate to your child's own life.
   - As your child completes the puzzles, look back together at the puzzles he or she has finished. Review the Bible stories and verses.

This Bible learning time at home will create a solid foundation for your child as he or she begins to read the Bible for him- or herself. The hours spent on the puzzles and Bible learning will help you and your child build a relationship that will be remembered long after the puzzles are all completed.

Academic Skills and *The Big Book of Kindergarten Puzzles #2*

Because *The Big Book of Kindergarten Puzzles #2* is primarily for kindergartners, these puzzles were created to challenge and aid kindergartners in the acquisition of the same academic skills they are learning in their kindergarten classrooms. The puzzles in *The Big Book of Kindergarten Puzzles #2* become progressively more difficult through the book, mirroring the same number, alphabet, logic, spatial and visual identification skills kindergartners are being taught through the school year. And all this is occurring while the puzzles reinforce biblical values and review important Bible stories and verses.

On page 220 of this book, you will find an index that categorizes puzzles according to academic skills. Puzzles may be chosen according to the skills presented but should also be used in sequence as much as possible. Puzzles 1-79 were created to be used with children beginning in the fall of their kindergarten year and ending in the spring with the completion of their kindergarten experience. Puzzles 80-104 are more general in the skills required (number and letter knowledge, etc.) and can be used during the summer both as a preview of skills for children entering kindergarten and a reinforcement for kindergarten graduates.

Because of the wide variance in the skill level of all kindergartners (depending on location, economic status, preschool attendance and English as a first language), these puzzles attempt to hit the median range. Your guidance will be an important part of helping a less-skilled child succeed at these puzzles. You can also challenge a more-skilled child by using the tips and hints below.

If the Puzzles Seem Too Difficult for Your Kindergartner

- Go over the directions one-on-one with the child. Have the child complete the first step as you watch and encourage him or her.
- Point out the visual helps included on the page (number lines, alphabet lines or dotted example lines to trace).
- In later puzzles, some of these visual helps no longer appear because the majority of kindergartners have internalized these skills. Write a simple number line or dotted example for a child who is still struggling.
- Leave pressure to perform out of the activity. If a puzzle seems too frustrating, give the child a blank sheet of paper and a hint about something to draw that is related to the Bible story or life-application idea. This will leave the child more eager to attempt a puzzle next time.

If the Puzzles Seem Too Easy for Your Kindergartner

- Point out and read the Bonus Idea to a child who quickly completes a puzzle. Be available to do this as soon as a child is finished with the main puzzle in order to retain the child's interest.
- The Bonus Ideas are generally open-ended, keeping a child engaged as long as he or she desires. To extend the child's involvement, invite a child to tell you about his or her Bonus Idea drawing or puzzle creation.
- For an extra challenge, white-out any example lines or number lines before photocopying puzzles. Or add your own Bonus Idea for children to complete by incorporating specific skills you know your kindergartner is working on.
- Be realistic about the time allotted to these puzzle book activities. Do not expect kindergartners to be engaged in a pencil and paper activity longer than 7 to 10 minutes.

The best learning occurs when an attentive adult is available to answer questions, guide conversation and activity, and be a real, live model of the biblical values these puzzles teach.

Tips for Teachers and Parents

1. Create a supply box for children to use with the puzzles. Include the following in the box:

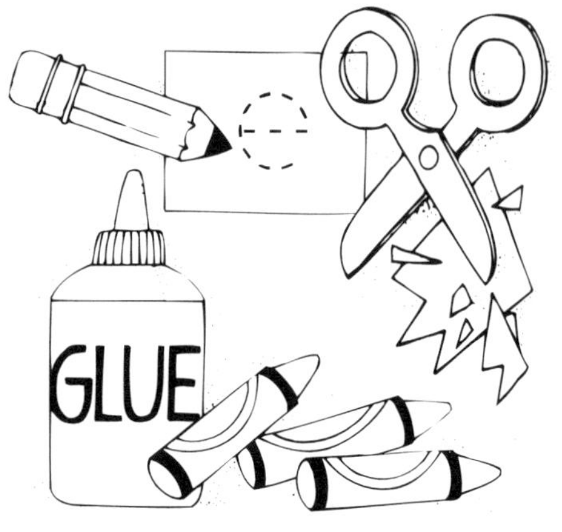

- Pencils and copies of the puzzle(s) you have selected
- Crayons, colored pencils or markers for coloring the puzzles
- Scissors and glue sticks for completion of some puzzles
- Extra sheets of blank paper for use with Bonus Ideas (if backs of puzzles are not used for this purpose)

2. Be available to participate in the learning process.

- Help children figure out what to do on the puzzle page: read the directions and/or give feedback on their completed work.
- Make sure to read aloud the short sentences that link the puzzle to the Bible story, Bible verse or life-application idea. Help children apply the Bible story or verse to their own lives. For example, children may name specific ways to show God's love by helping friends or family members.

3. Help your children enjoy the puzzles.

- Many kindergartners are naturally drawn to puzzles and mazes. Reinforce this by communicating that completing the puzzles is a fun challenge and is helping them grow into the people God has planned for them to be.
- Use praise and encouragement to motivate a child who is working on a puzzle. For example, "Katie, I see you have crossed out all the upper-cased letters. Good work!" or "Seth, I can tell you are working hard to find the hidden objects."
- Consider placing a sticker or stamp on each completed puzzle.
- Display completed puzzles on a bulletin board in the classroom or on the refrigerator door at home.
- If a child is not interested in a certain puzzle, tell him or her about the Bonus Idea. If the Bonus Idea fails to interest the child, provide the child with blank paper on which to draw. Challenge the child to draw something about the day's Bible story. For example, for the story of Noah, children draw as many pairs of animals as they can.
- Most children find it easy to occupy themselves by drawing. Even if their artwork does not relate to the Bible story, point out that they are using their God-given gifts of eyes, hands and fingers. Staying positive will help your children to be more willing to try puzzles in the future.

Count all the different kinds of things God created.
Fill in the chart below.

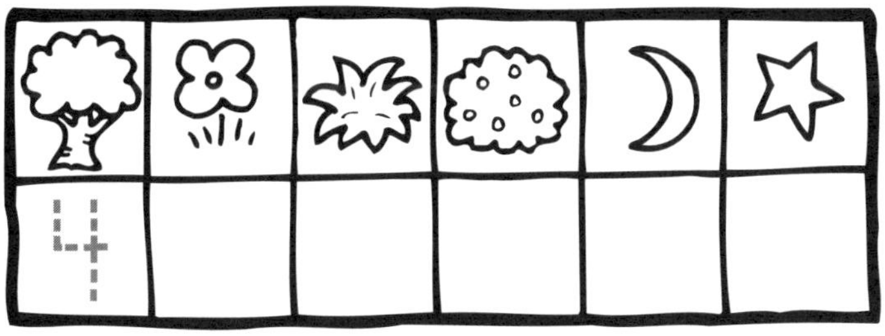

1 2 3 4 5 6

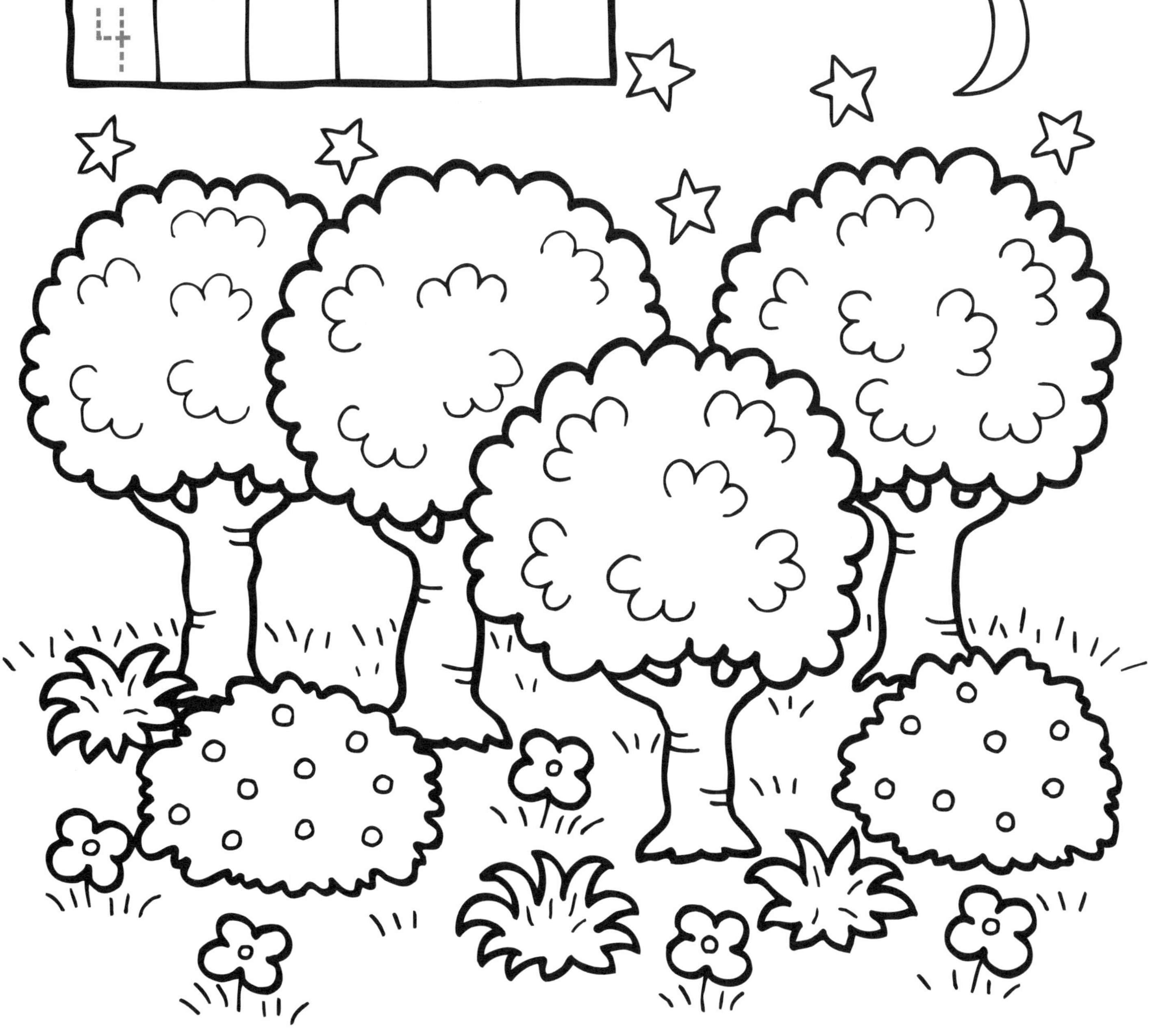

4					

We can thank God for making the sea, the land and the trees.
Our Bible says, "God made the world and everything in it." (See Acts 17:24.)

Draw other flowers and stars in the picture.

Trace each shape with your finger and say its name.

circle **triangle**

Color the ○s YELLOW. Color the △s GREEN.

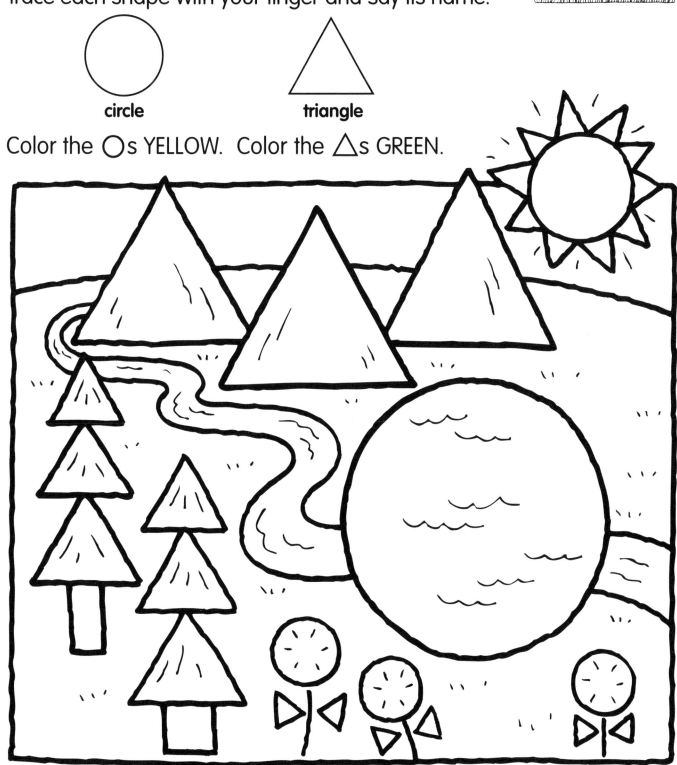

We can thank God for making mountains, flowers and lakes.
Our Bible says, "God made the world and everything in it." (See Acts 17:24.)

Find the □ and the ▯.
square **rectangle**

In each group, draw an ✖ on the one that doesn't belong.

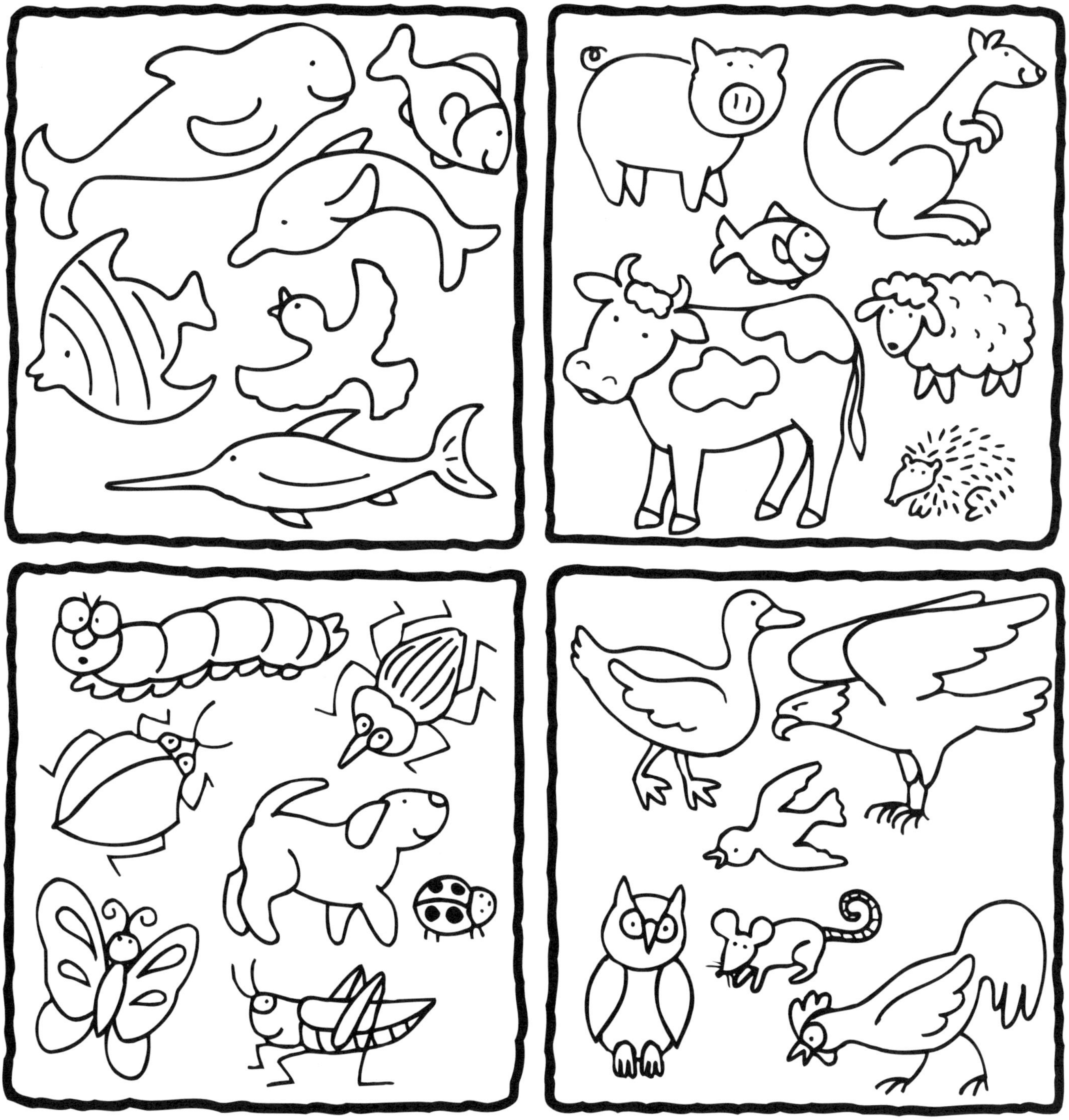

God made all the animals in the world.
Our Bible says, "God saw all that he had made, and it was very good." Genesis 1:31

How many fish are there? ________

How many birds are there? ________

Draw a line to match each animal with its tail.

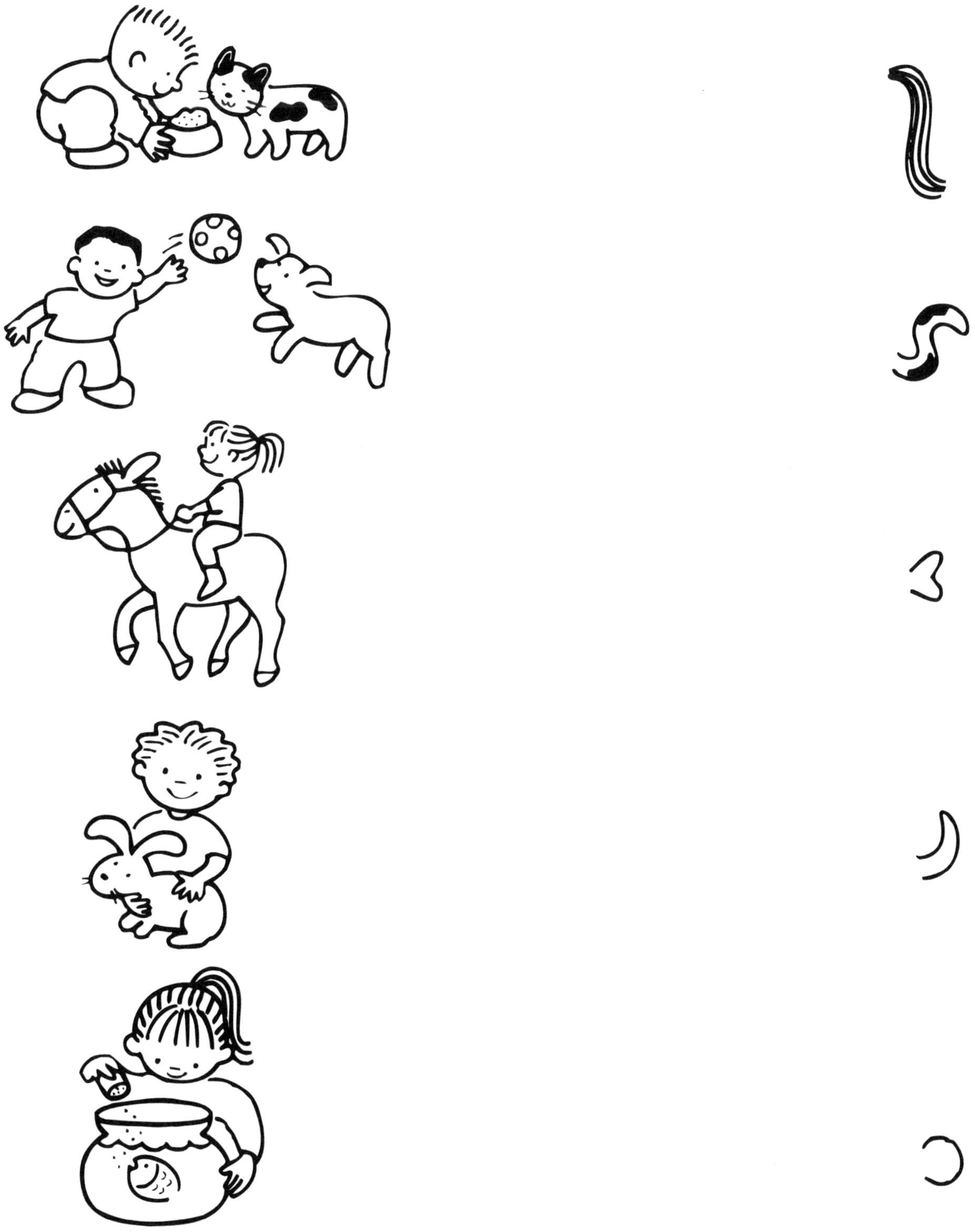

We can be thankful for all the animals God made.
Our Bible says, "God saw all that he had made, and it was very good." Genesis 1:31

What animal are you thankful God made? Draw a picture of it!

Help Adam find Eve in the garden.

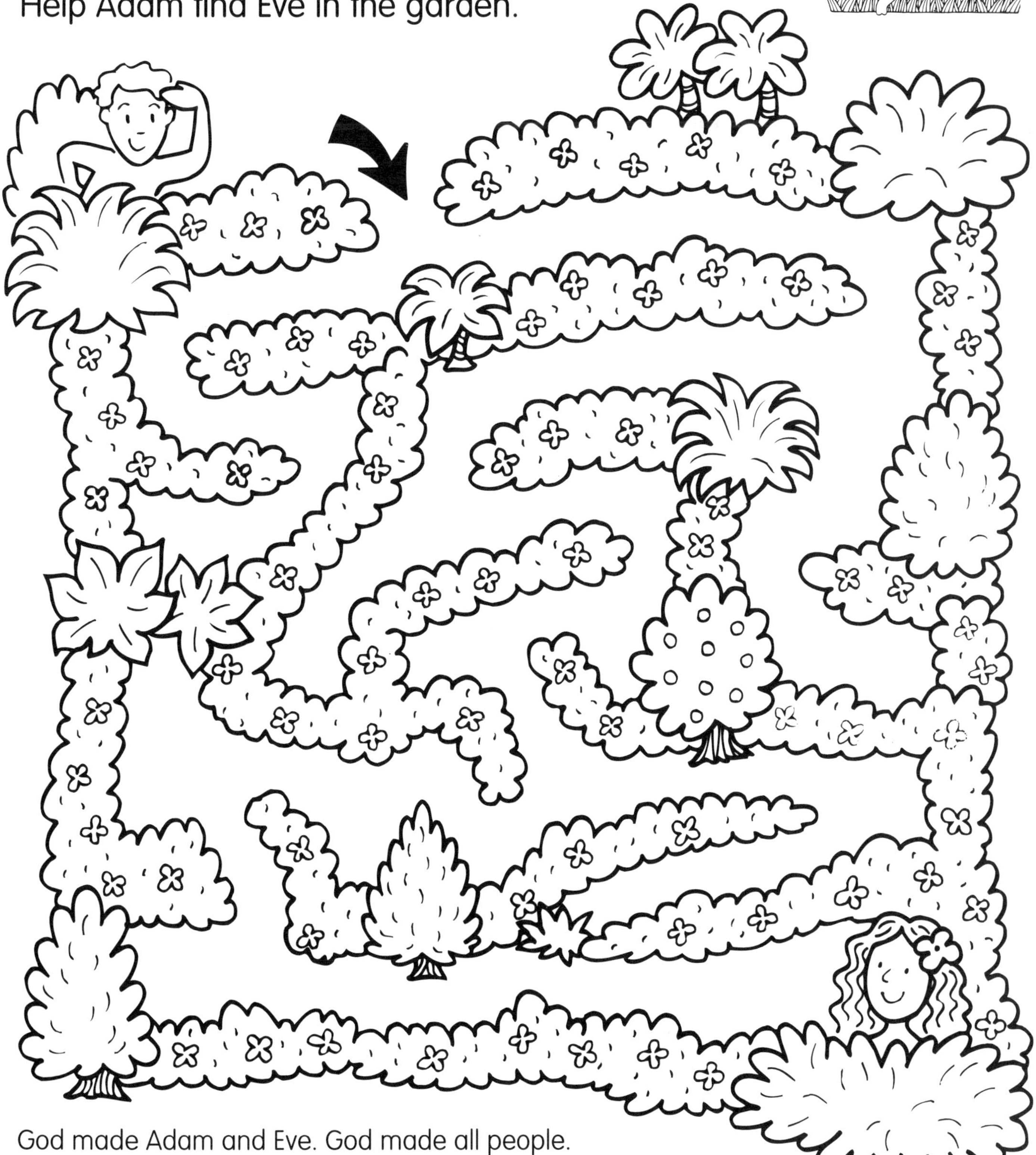

God made Adam and Eve. God made all people.
We can thank God that He made us!
Our Bible says, "Pray always and be thankful." (See Colossians 4:2.)

Draw a picture of a garden you would like to live in.

Cut apart the squares. Then put them together to make a picture of two people God made!

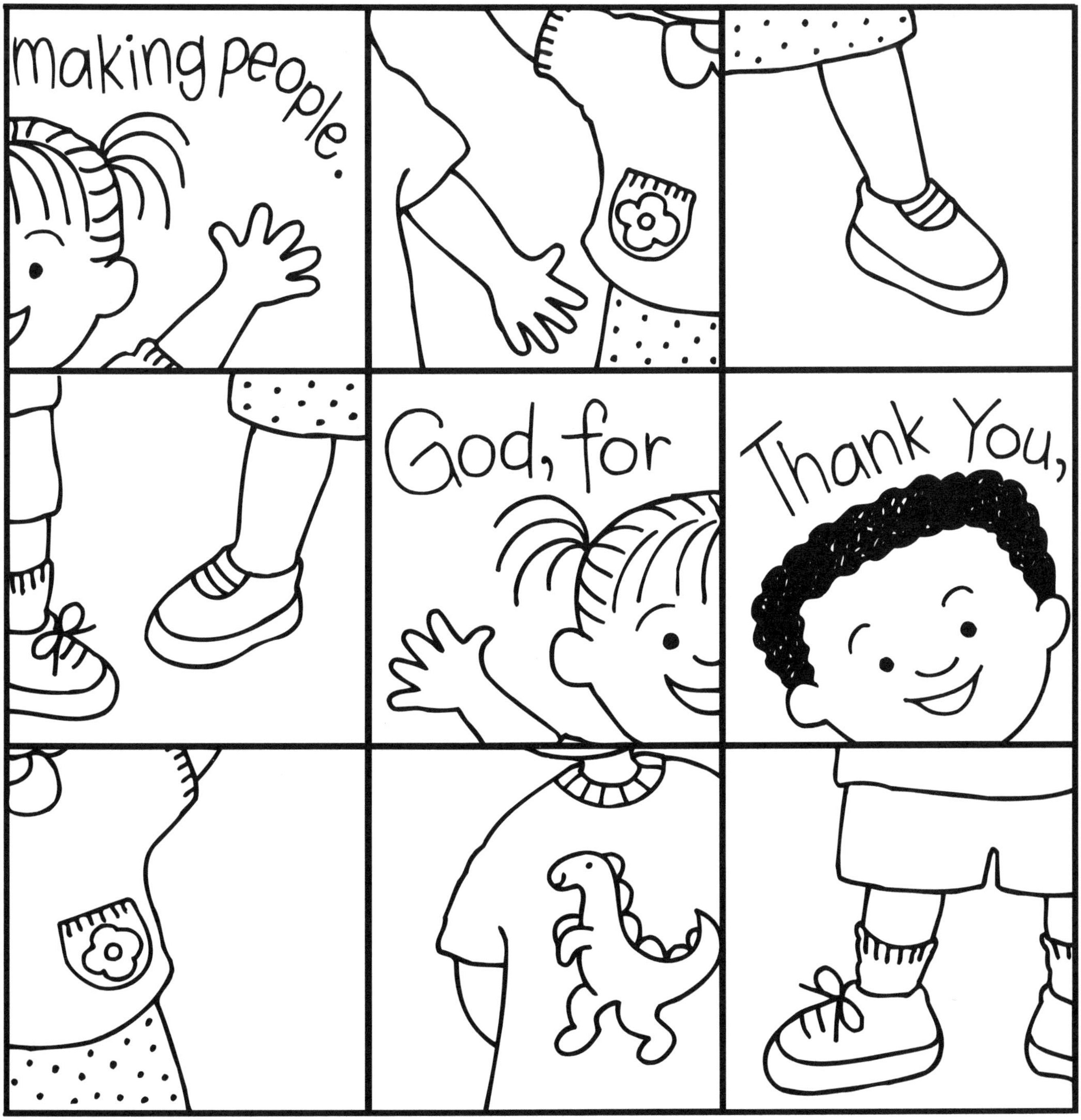

making people.

God, for

Thank You,

God made us!

We can thank God that He made all people.

Our Bible says, "Pray always and be thankful." (See Colossians 4:2.)

Glue the finished picture to a sheet of paper.

Draw a ○ around the biggest picture in each row.

God loved Adam and Eve, even when they did wrong.
We can thank God for loving us and sending Jesus.
Our Bible says, "God has sent his Son to be the Savior of the world." (See 1 John 4:14.)

Make an ✖ on the smallest picture in each row.
Color the middle-sized picture in each row.

Color the boy's 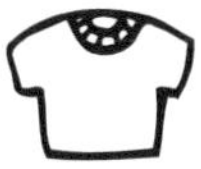 GREEN.

Color the boy's 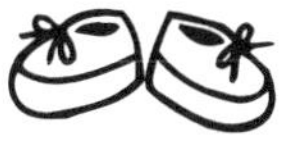 BROWN.

Trace the letters to find the name of who the boy is thankful for.

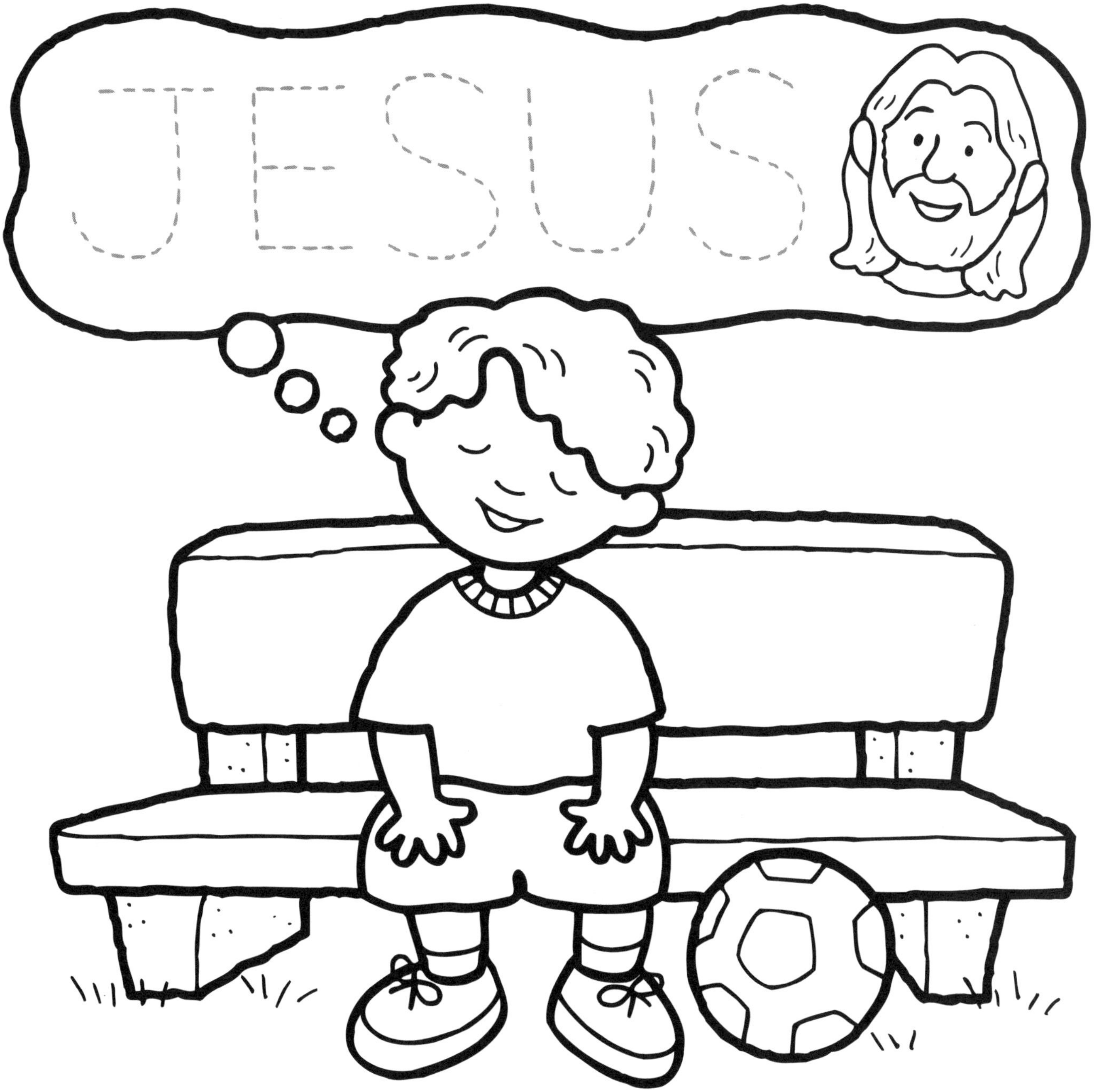

JESUS

We can thank God for loving us and sending Jesus.
Our Bible says, "God has sent his Son to be the Savior of the world." (See 1 John 4:14.)

Who sent Jesus? Follow the code to fill in the blank lines.

______ ______ ______

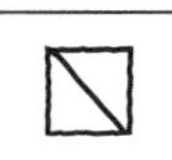  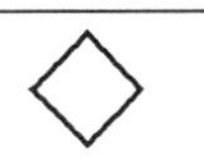

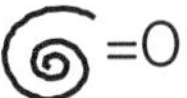=O 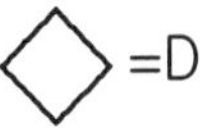=D 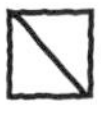 =G

Connect the dots to see what Noah built.

1	2	3	4	5	6	7	8	9	10	11	12	13	14	15

14 13

15 2 11 12 1

4 3 10 9

5 8

6 7

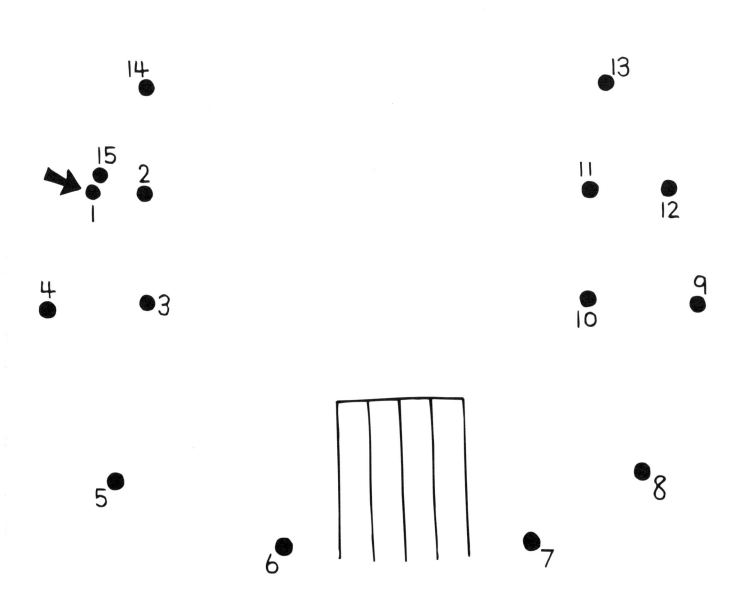

God told Noah to build a boat. Noah obeyed.
We can do good and obey God, too. God will help us.
Our Bible says, "God made us to do good." (See Ephesians 2:10.)

Draw water for the ark to float on. Draw some animals in the ark.

Draw a line to match the puzzle pieces that show ways to obey God.

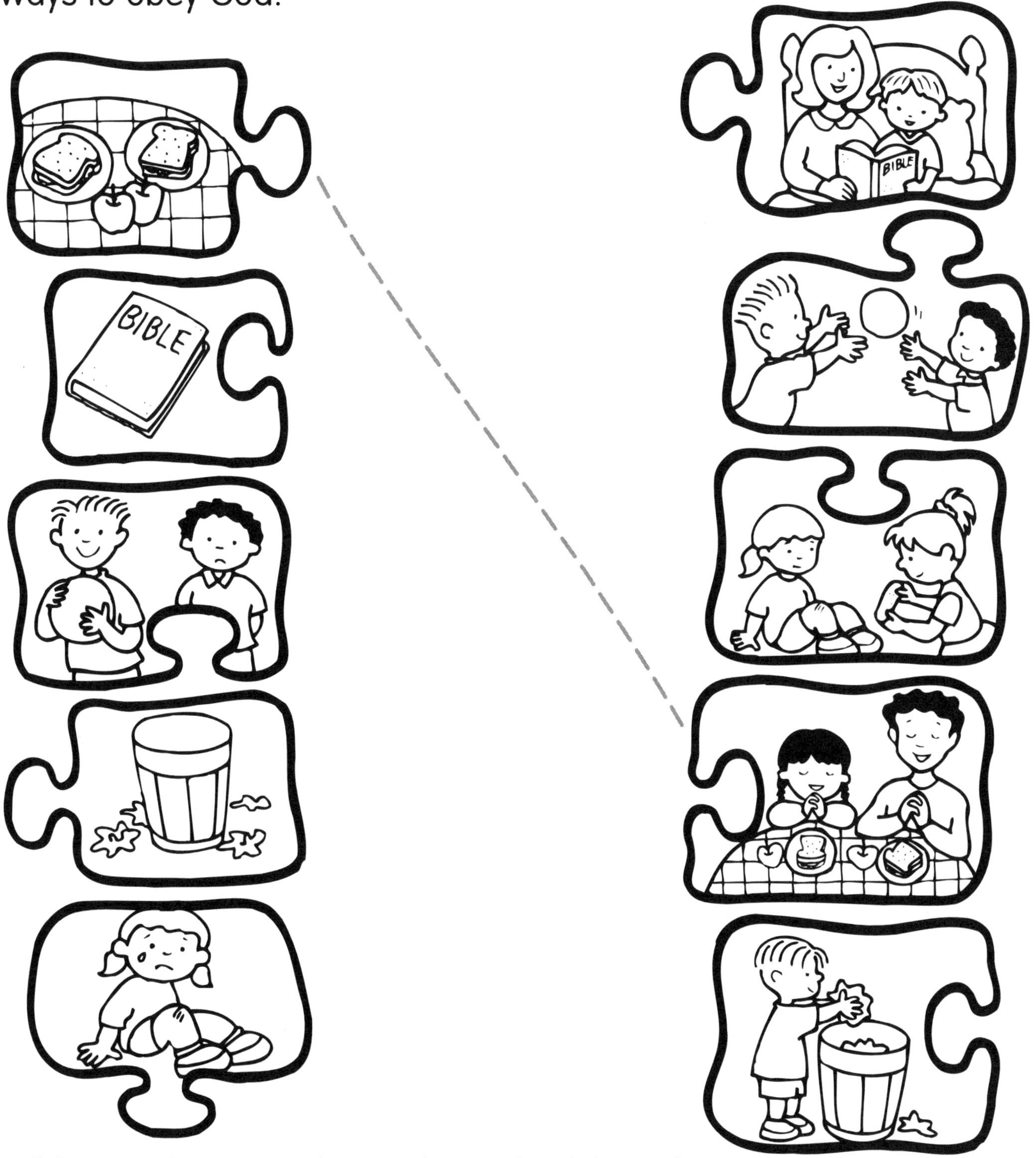

Tell the ways the pictures show to obey God and do good.
Our Bible says, "God made us to do good." (See Ephesians 2:10.)

Draw a ★ by a way you have obeyed God.
Draw a ○ around a way you can obey God this week.

In each row, write the missing number on the animal.

1 2 3 4 5 6 7 8 9 10 11 12

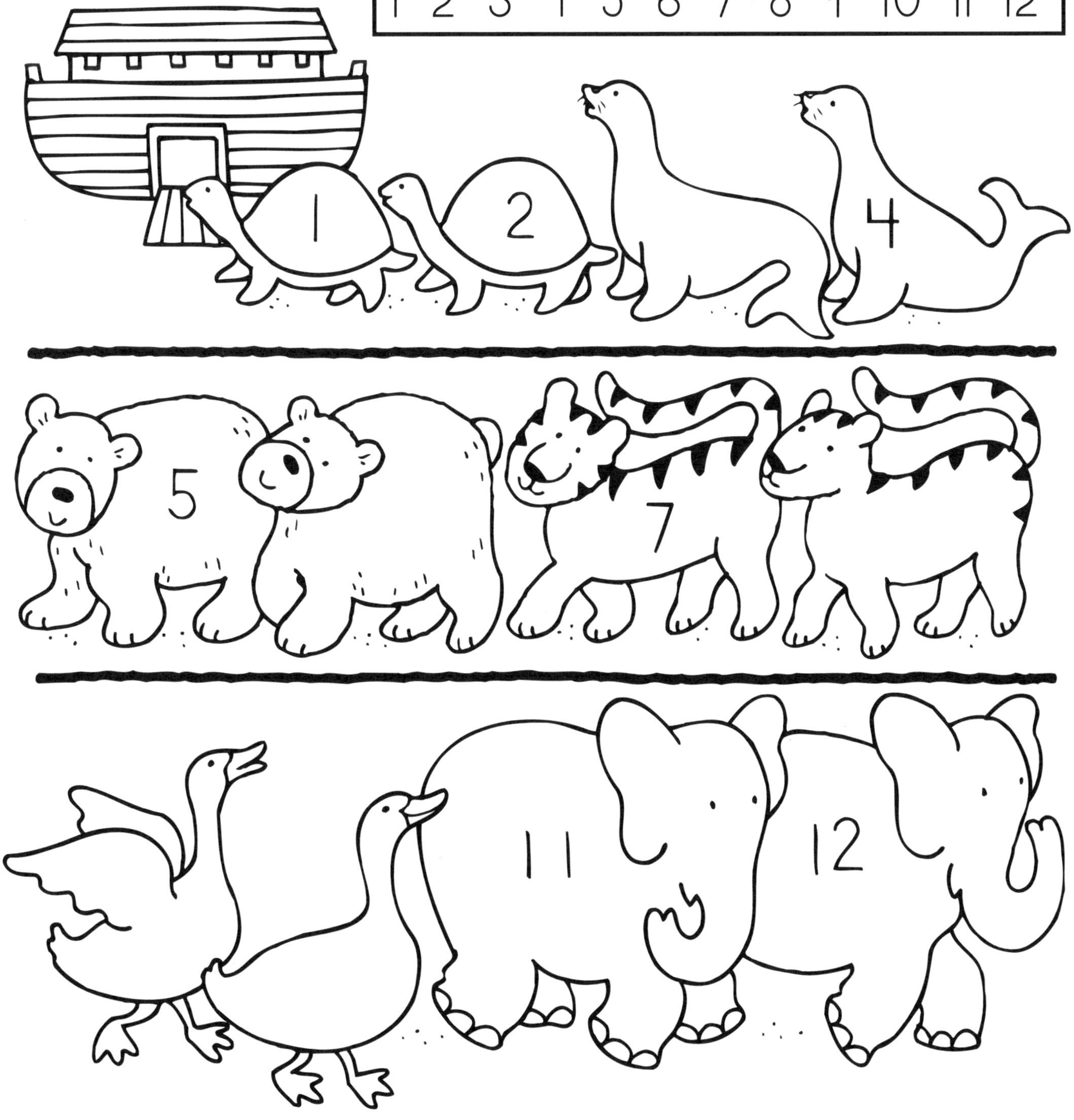

1 2 4

5 7

11 12

God helped Noah get all the animals on the boat.
God helps us do good.
Our Bible says, "Do what is right and good." Deuteronomy 6:18

Count all the animals on this page.

Write that number. ______

Trace each shape.

square   circle   triangle   rectangle

Find each shape in one of the pictures of a child doing a good thing. Draw a line to connect the matching shapes.

God helps us do good.
Our Bible says, "Do what is right and good." Deuteronomy 6:18

Draw a picture with a □, ○, △ or ▭ in it.
Try to draw all 4 shapes in your picture.

Draw an ✖ on all the silly things in this picture.
(There are at least 7.)
Draw a ○ around the people taking care of the animals.

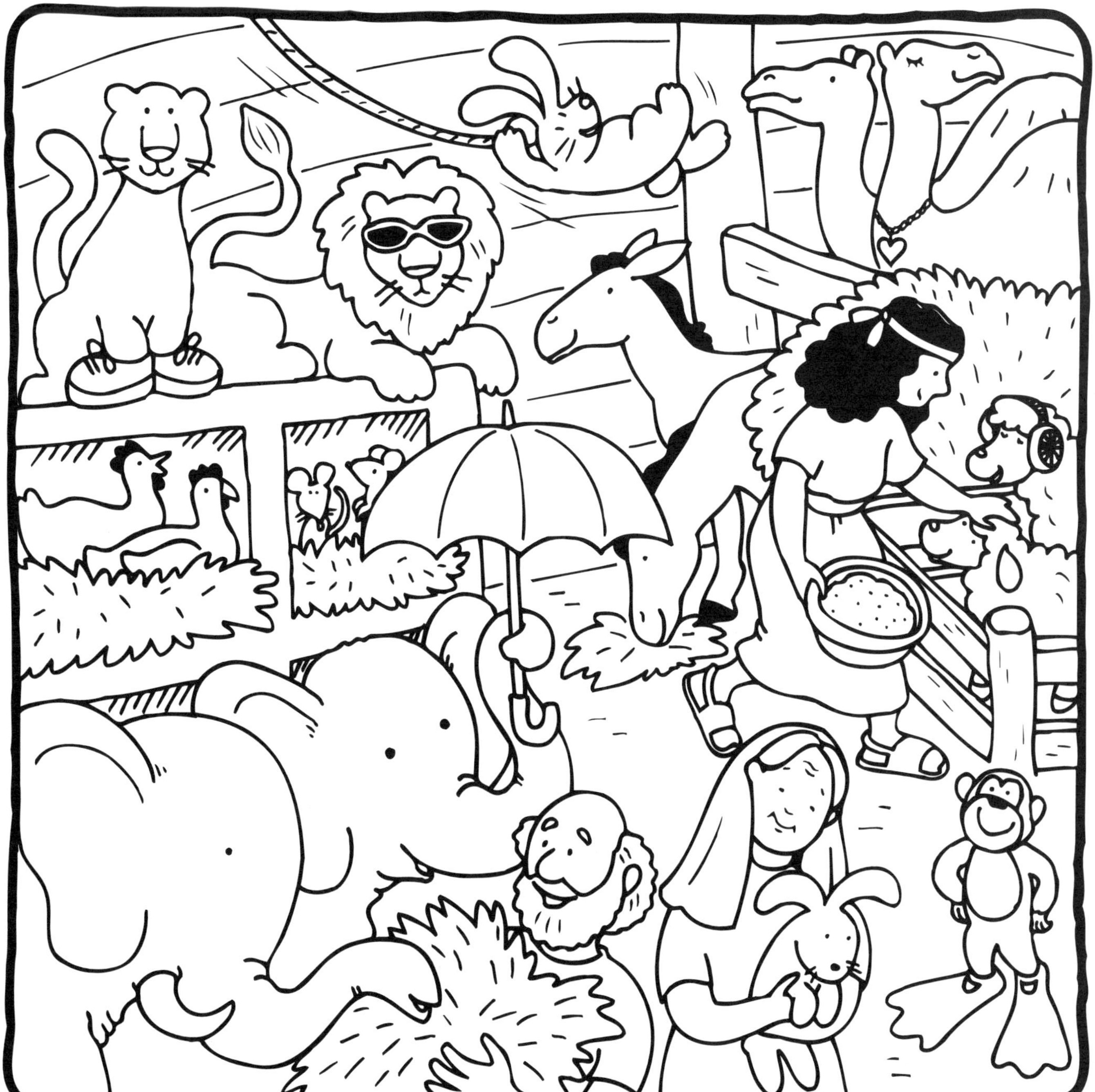

Noah and his family took care of the animals on the boat.
Our Bible says, "Whatever you do, do your work for the Lord." (See Colossians 3:23.)

How many **pairs** of animals are on the boat?
(A pair is 2 of the same kind.)
Color each **pair** the same color.

Draw a line from each object in the middle to the picture where it is needed.

Ketchup

When we help others, we show that we love God.
Our Bible says, "Whatever you do, do your work for the Lord." (See Colossians 3:23.)

Draw a picture of what you can do to help someone in your family.

Count the number of objects in each box.
Then write the number in the little □.
Draw a ★ in the box that has **more** than 5 objects.
(**More** means a bigger number.)

1 2 3 4 5 6 7 8

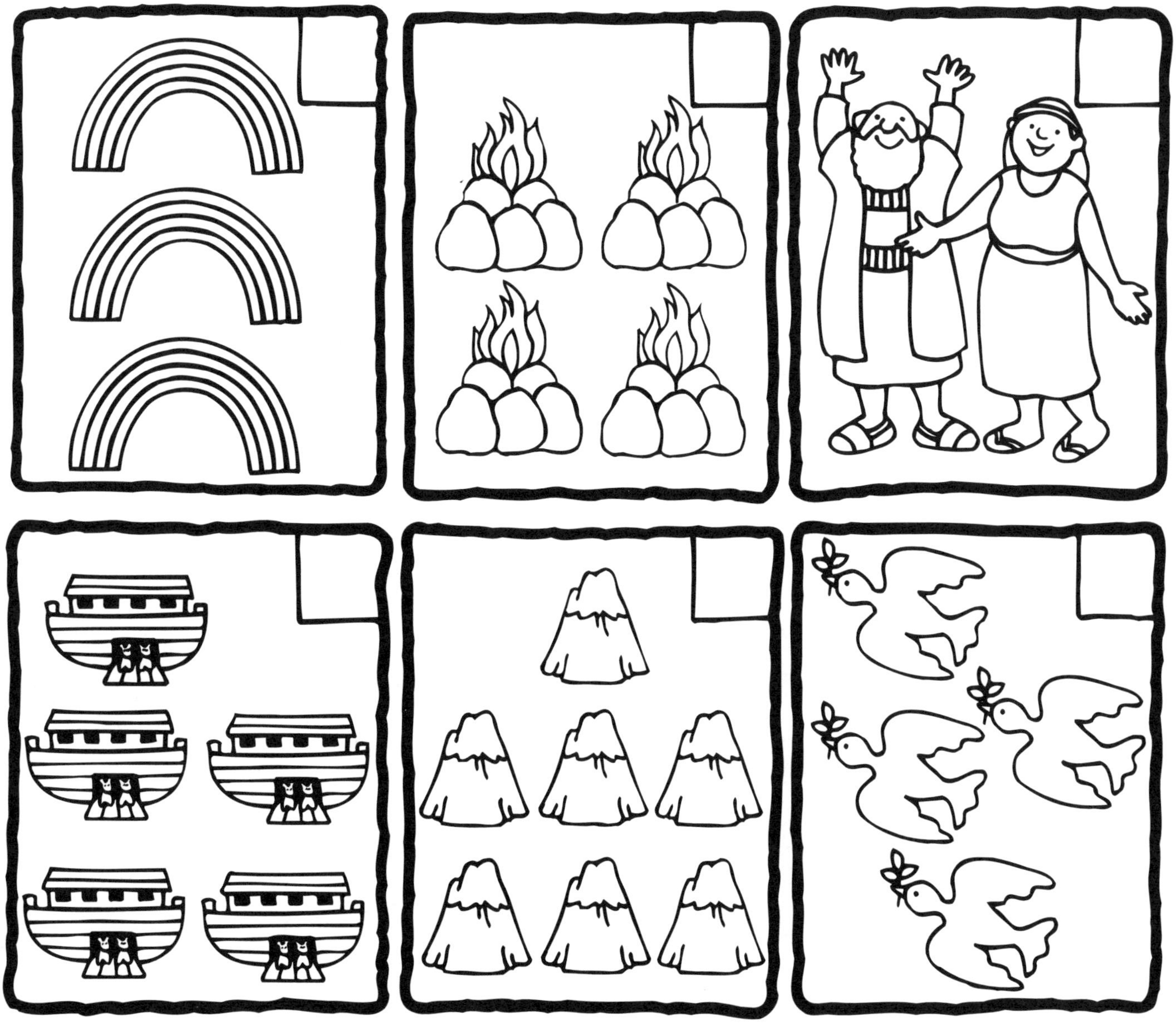

God put a rainbow in the sky to remind Noah and his family of God's love and help.
They thanked God. We can thank God for helping us, too.
Our Bible says, "God, we give you thanks." 1 Chronicles 29:13

Color the rainbows using **more** than 3 colors.
Draw a line between the boxes that have an **equal** number of objects.
(**Equal** means the same.)

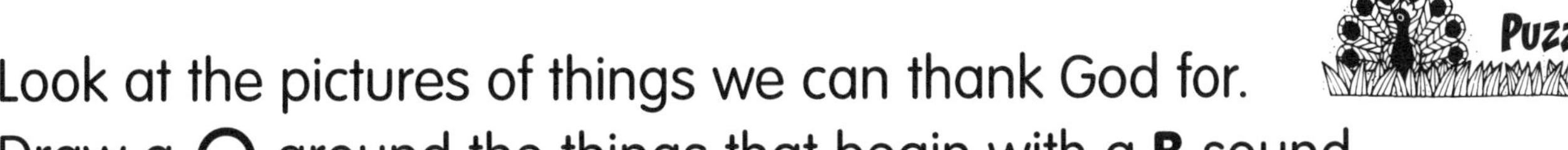

Look at the pictures of things we can thank God for.
Draw a ○ around the things that begin with a **B** sound.
Draw a □ around the things that begin with a **D** sound.

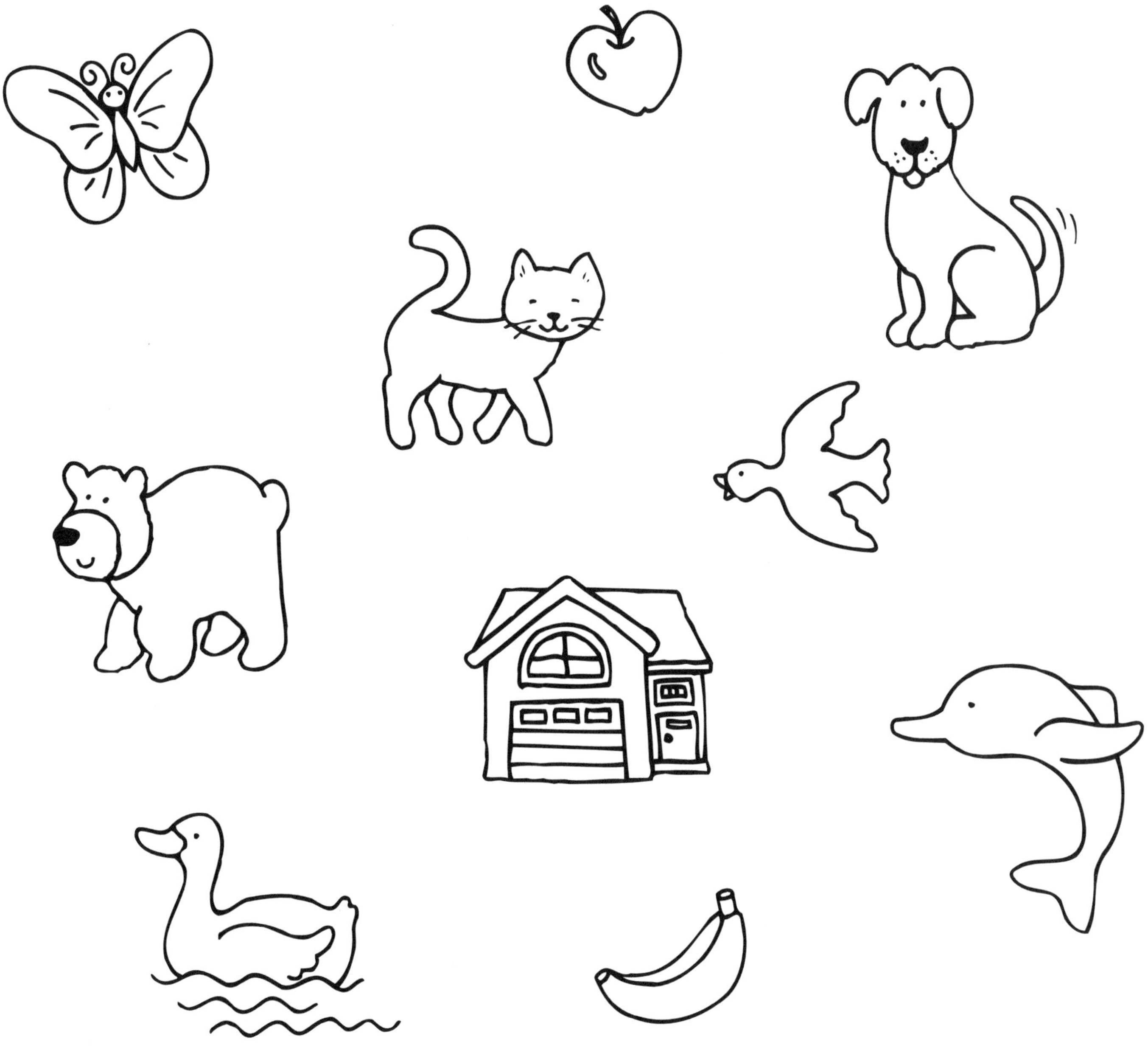

God helps us and gives us good things.
We can thank God for all that He gives us.
Our Bible says, "God, we give you thanks." 1 Chronicles 29:13

Color the **B** pictures BLUE.
Color the **D** pictures RED.
Write the beginning sound next to the leftover pictures.

Help Abraham find his tent.

Abraham obeyed God and went to a new land.
We can obey God, too.
Our Bible says, "Obey the Lord." Deuteronomy 27:10

BONUS IDEA! Color the camel that has black hooves.

In each row, cut apart the pictures.
Glue them in order on a separate sheet of paper.

How are the children in these pictures obeying God?
We can obey God, too.
Our Bible says, "Obey the Lord." Deuteronomy 27:10

Draw 3 pictures to tell a story about a way you can obey God when you are playing with a friend.

Count the animals on each hill.
Then write that number on the shepherd.

1 2 3 4 5 6 7 8 9 10

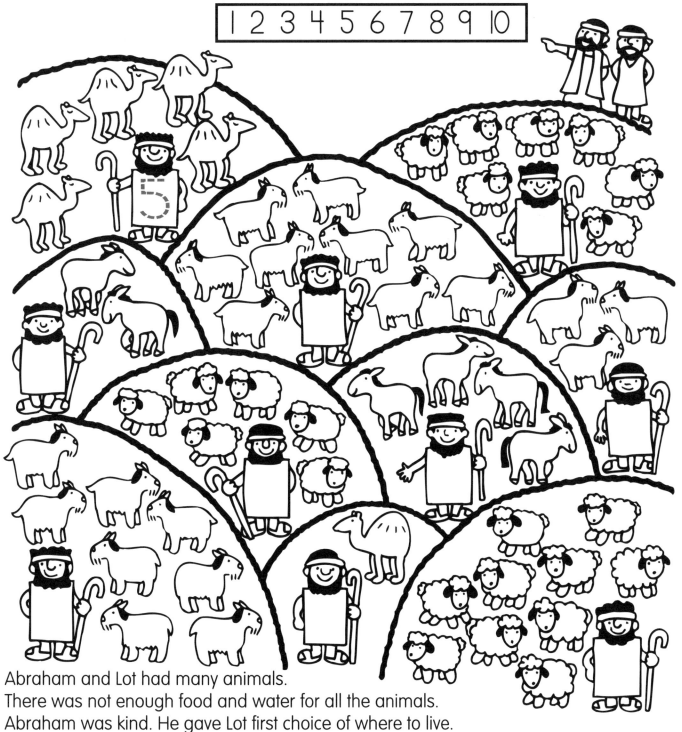

Abraham and Lot had many animals.
There was not enough food and water for all the animals.
Abraham was kind. He gave Lot first choice of where to live.
We can choose to be kind to others, too.
Our Bible says, "Do to others as you would have them do to you." Luke 6:31

Find the animal on each hill that is missing a tail. Draw in the tail.

Draw a line from each group of cookies to the plate with the correct number.

6

7

8

9

10

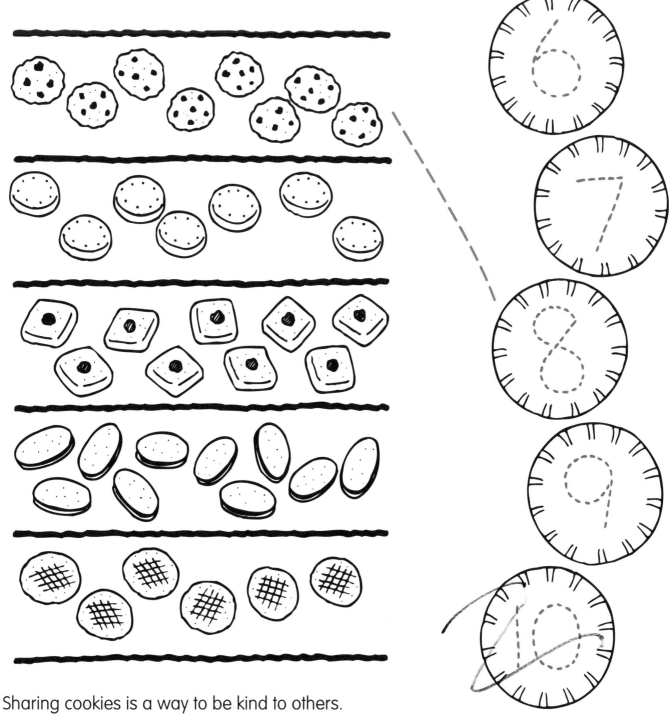

Sharing cookies is a way to be kind to others.
What else can you share with others to be kind to them?
Our Bible says, "Do to others as you would have them do to you." Luke 6:31

Draw a big plate. How many cookies can you draw to fit on it? _____

Draw a line from these objects to where they are in the picture of Abraham and his visitors.

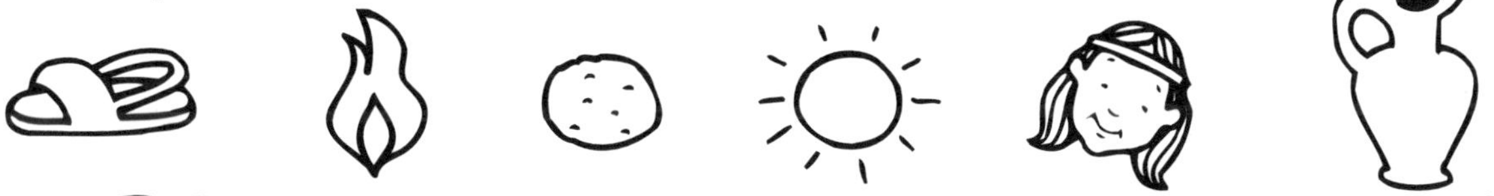

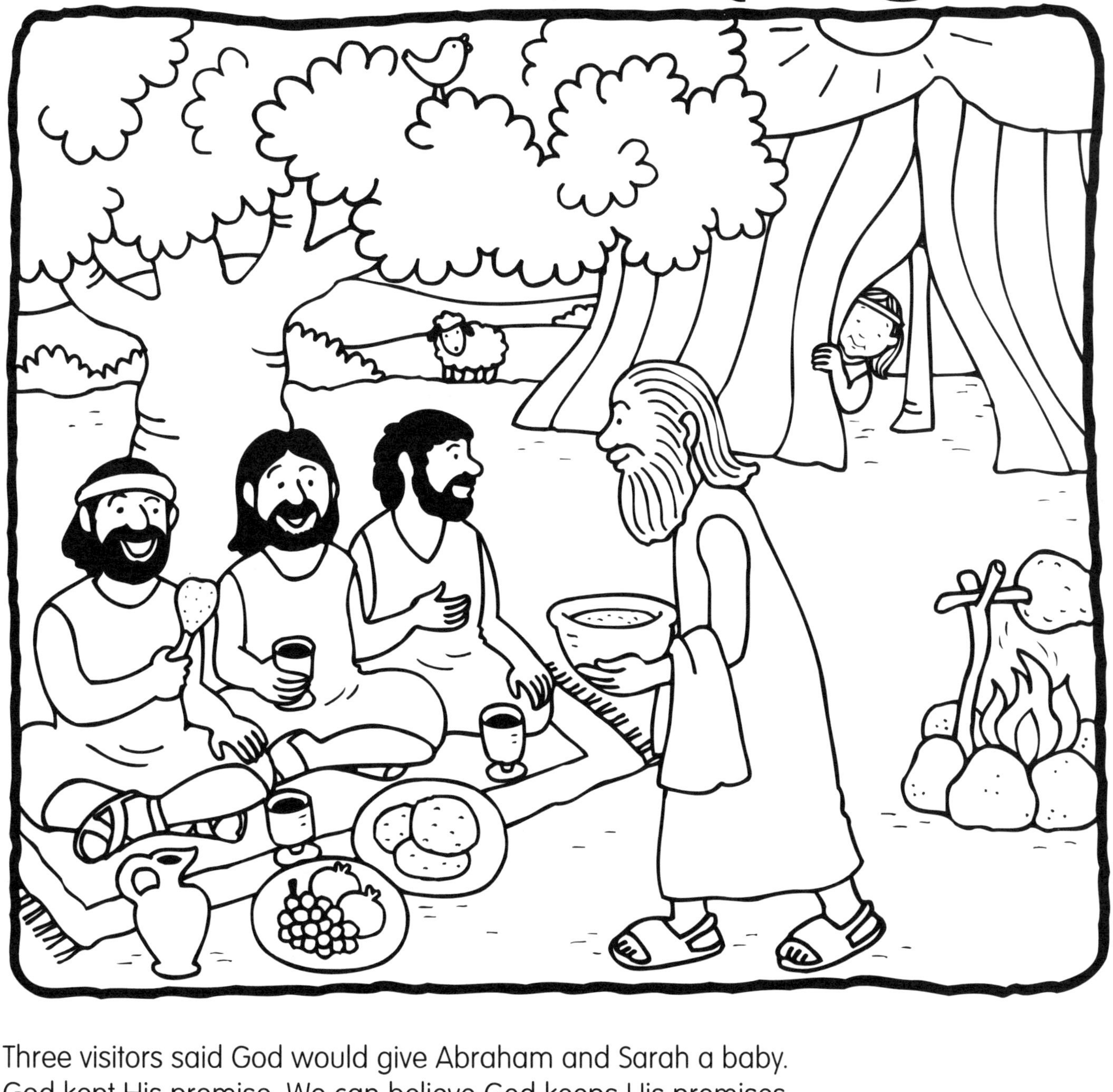

Three visitors said God would give Abraham and Sarah a baby. God kept His promise. We can believe God keeps His promises. Our Bible says, "I trust in God's word." (See Psalm 119:42.)

Draw a ○ around these objects in the picture:

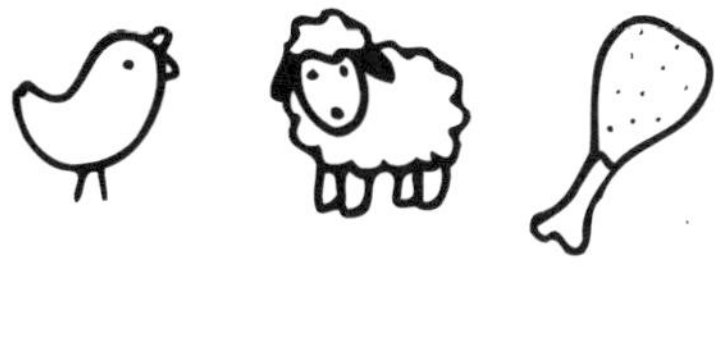

Find the shapes that are the same.
Then draw lines between the matching shapes to see where we can learn about God's promises.

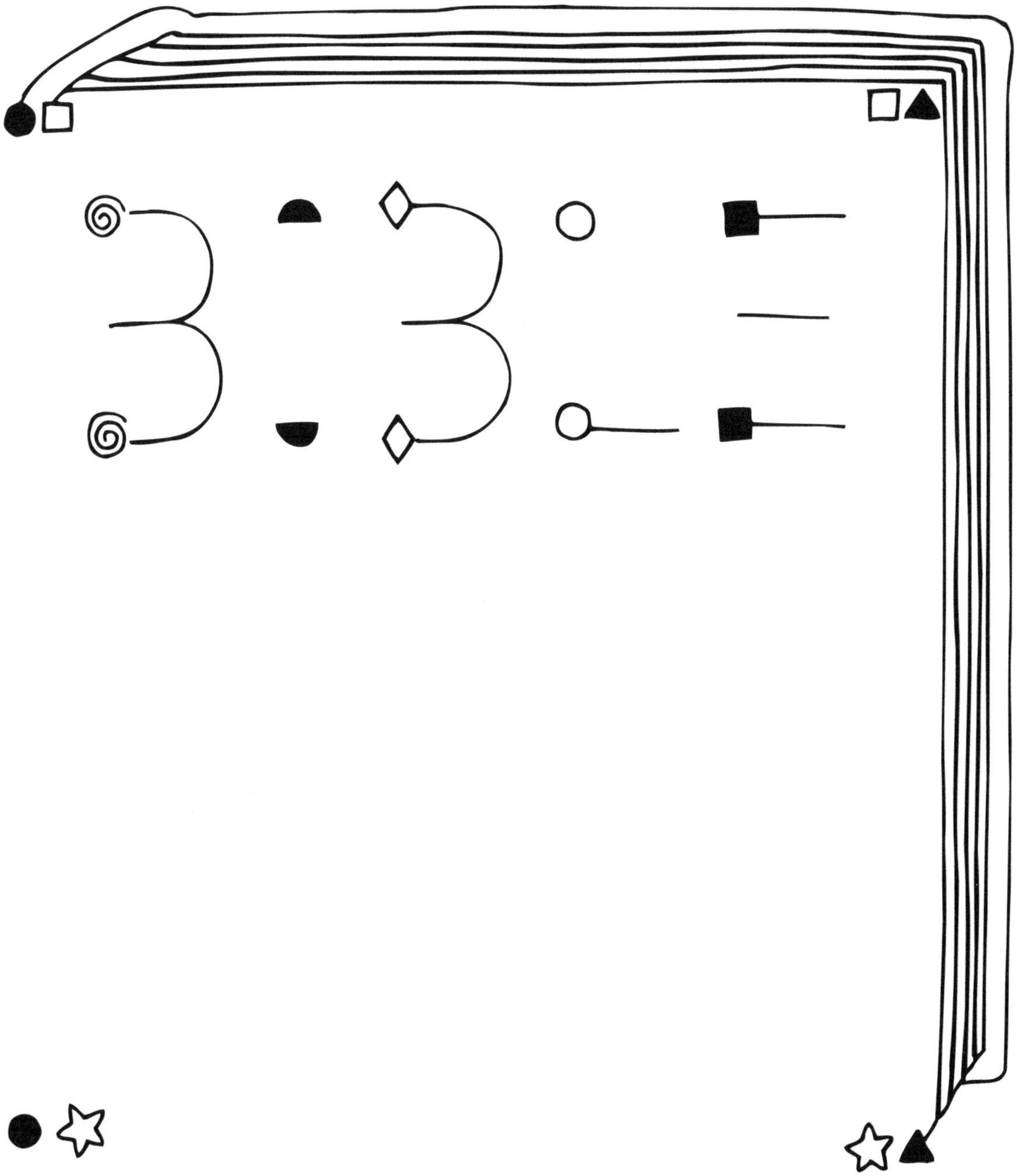

We learn about God's promises in the Bible.
We can believe God keeps His promises.
Our Bible says, "I trust in God's word." (See Psalm 119:42.)

Fold a sheet of paper to make a □.
Fold a sheet of paper to make a △.

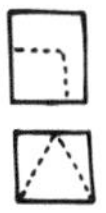

Color each ○ you find in this picture of Eliezer and Rebekah.

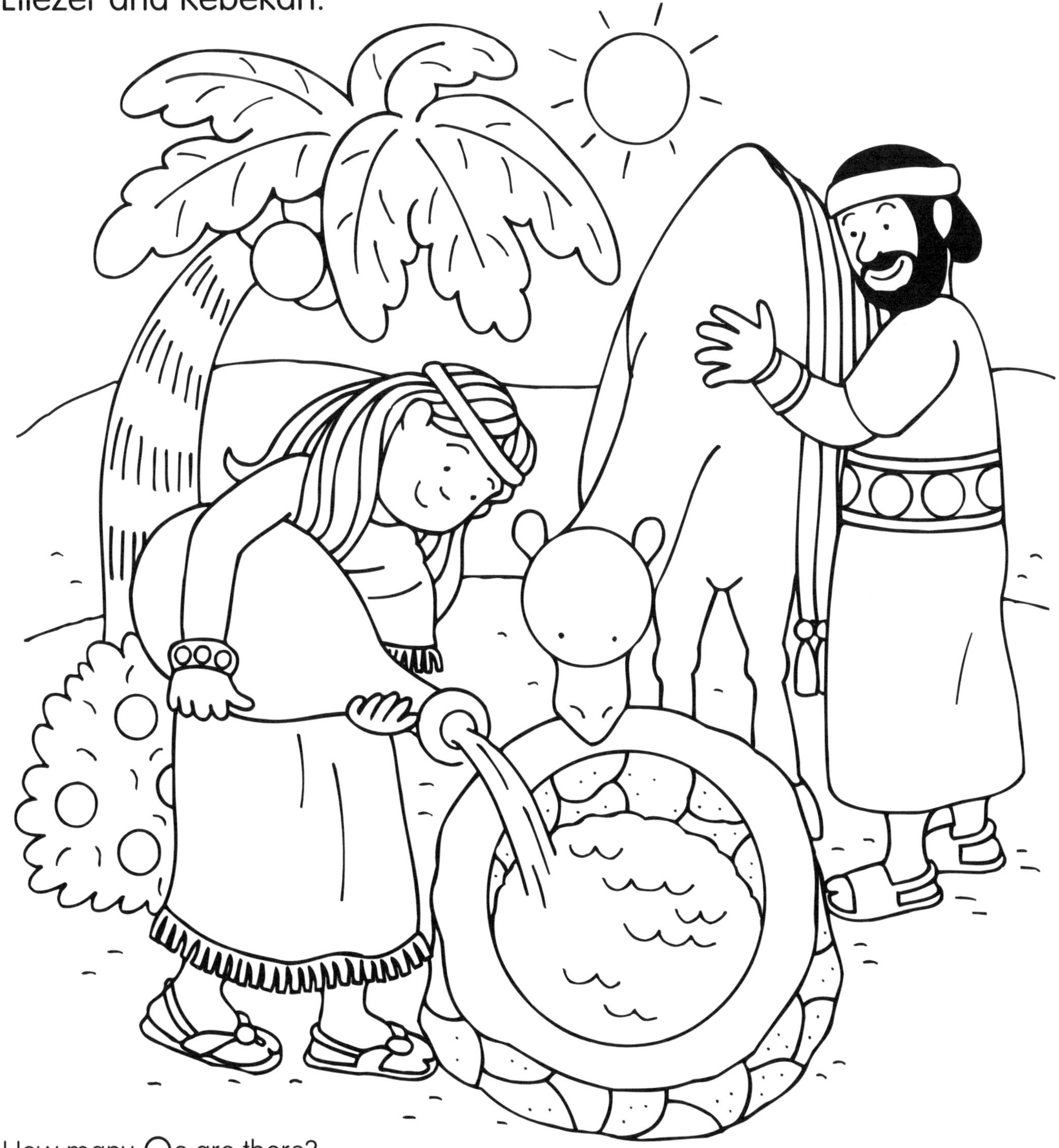

How many ○s are there? _______

Eliezer prayed. God helped Eliezer find Rebekah. We can pray to God, too. Our Bible says, "The Lord hears when I pray to him." (See Psalm 4:3.)

Draw a ★ by the BIGGEST ○.
Make a ✔ by the smallest ○s.

Draw lines to show how many of each object are in the girl's room.

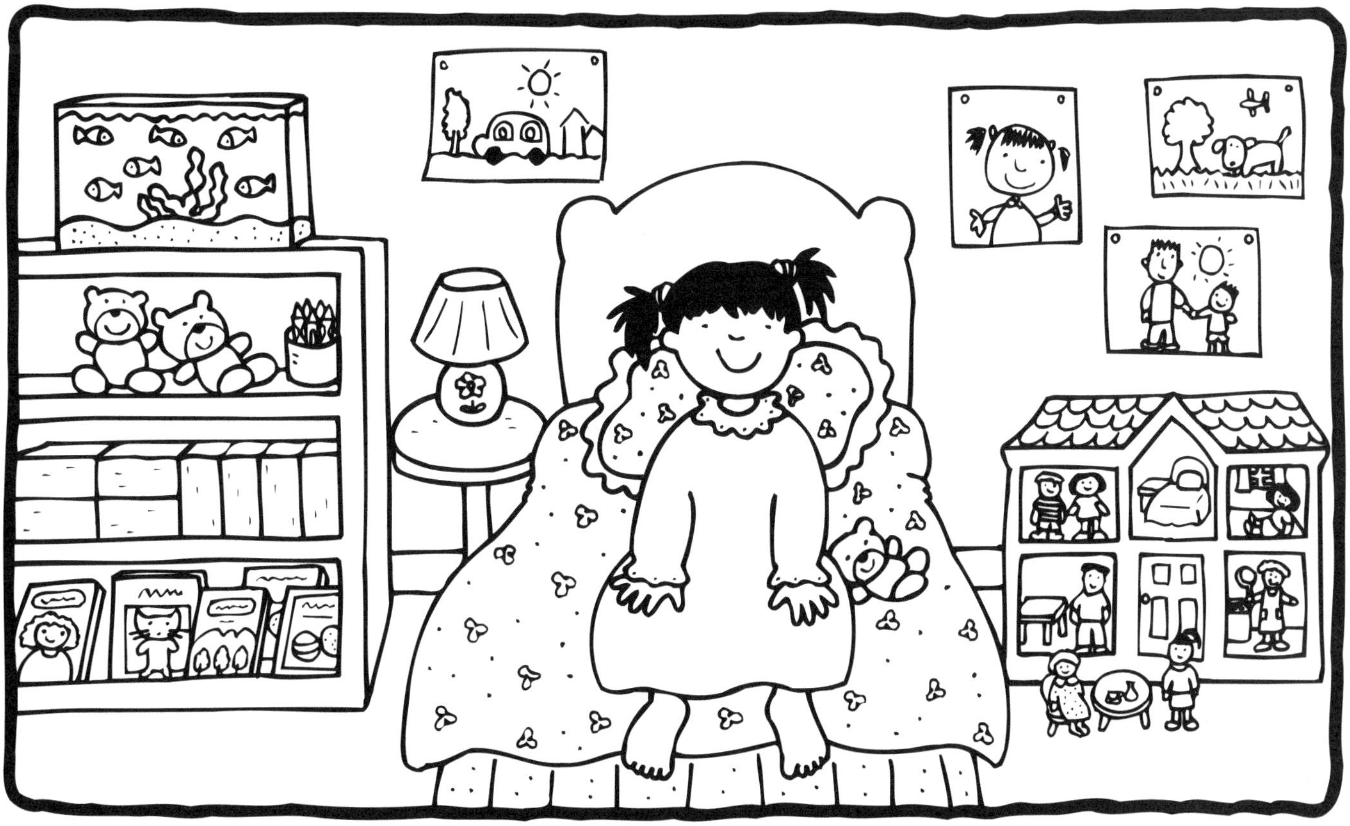

3 4 5 6 7 8

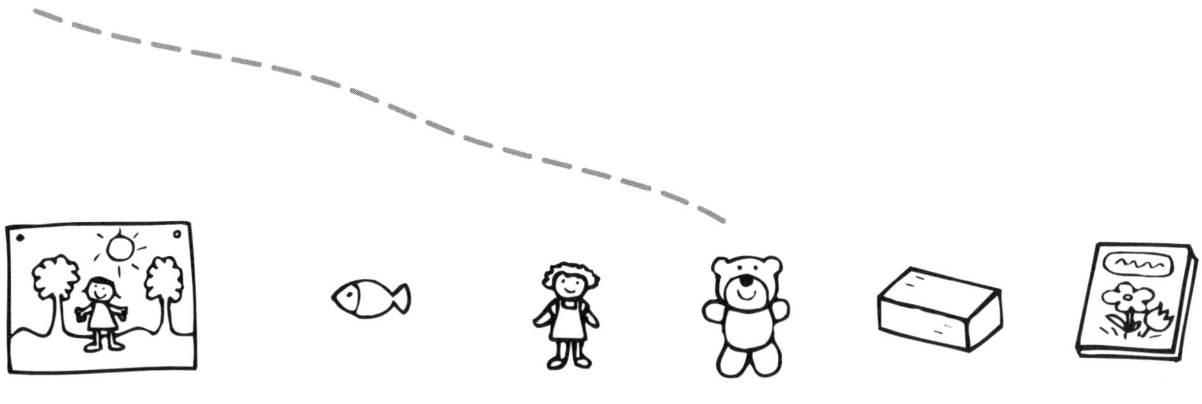

We can pray to God.
We can thank Him for the good things He gives us.
Our Bible says, "The Lord hears when I pray to him." (See Psalm 4:3.)

Draw a picture of something you want to thank God for.

There are 10 differences between these 2 pictures.
How many can you find?
Draw an ✖ on a number when you find a difference.

1	2	3	4	5	6	7	8	9	10

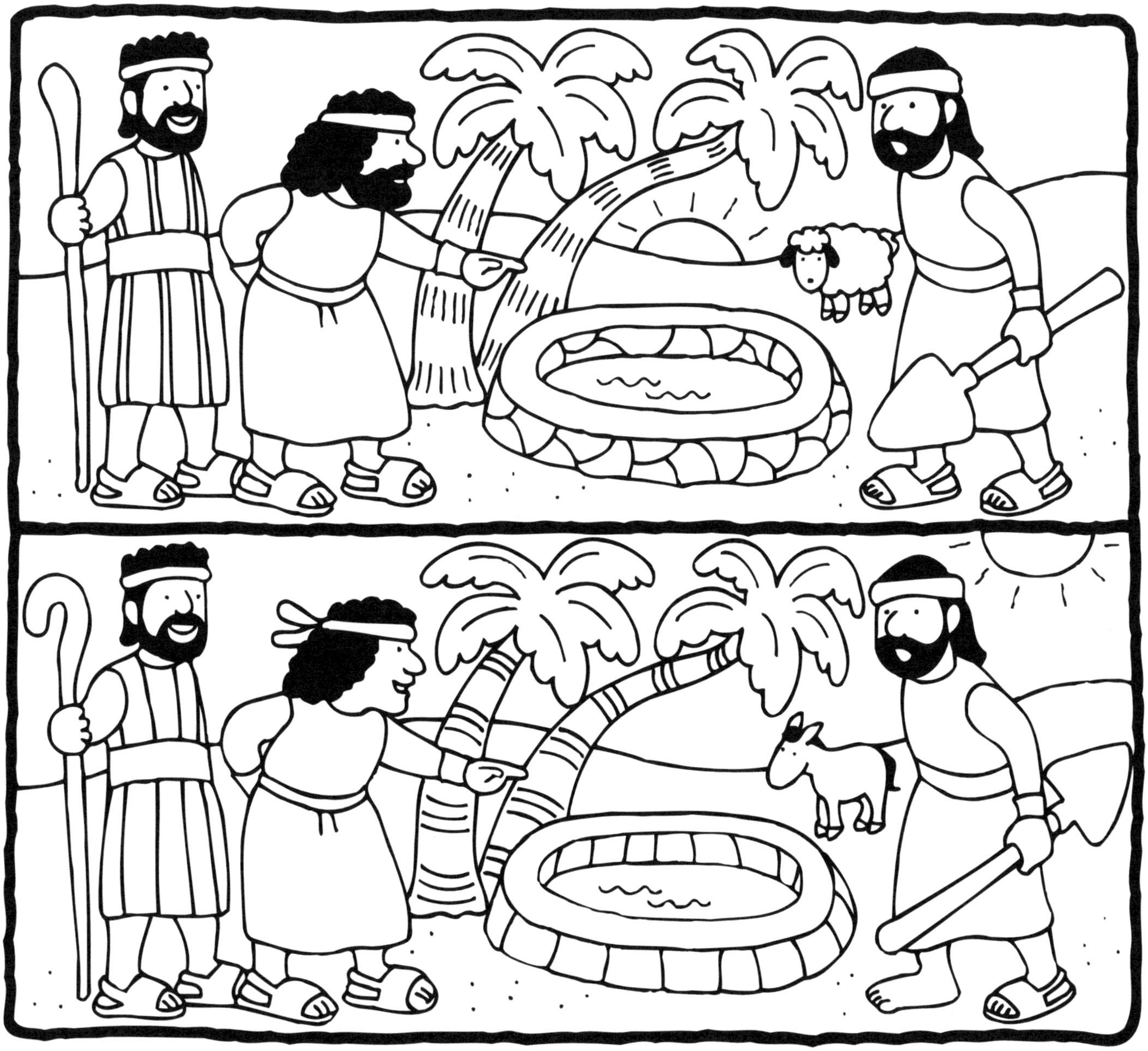

Isaac did not argue with the people who wanted his wells.
Isaac showed love. We can show love, too.
Our Bible says, "Love your neighbor." Matthew 22:39

What do Isaac and his helpers need in order to get water from the well? Draw it in the picture.

Trace each path to find out what happens next.

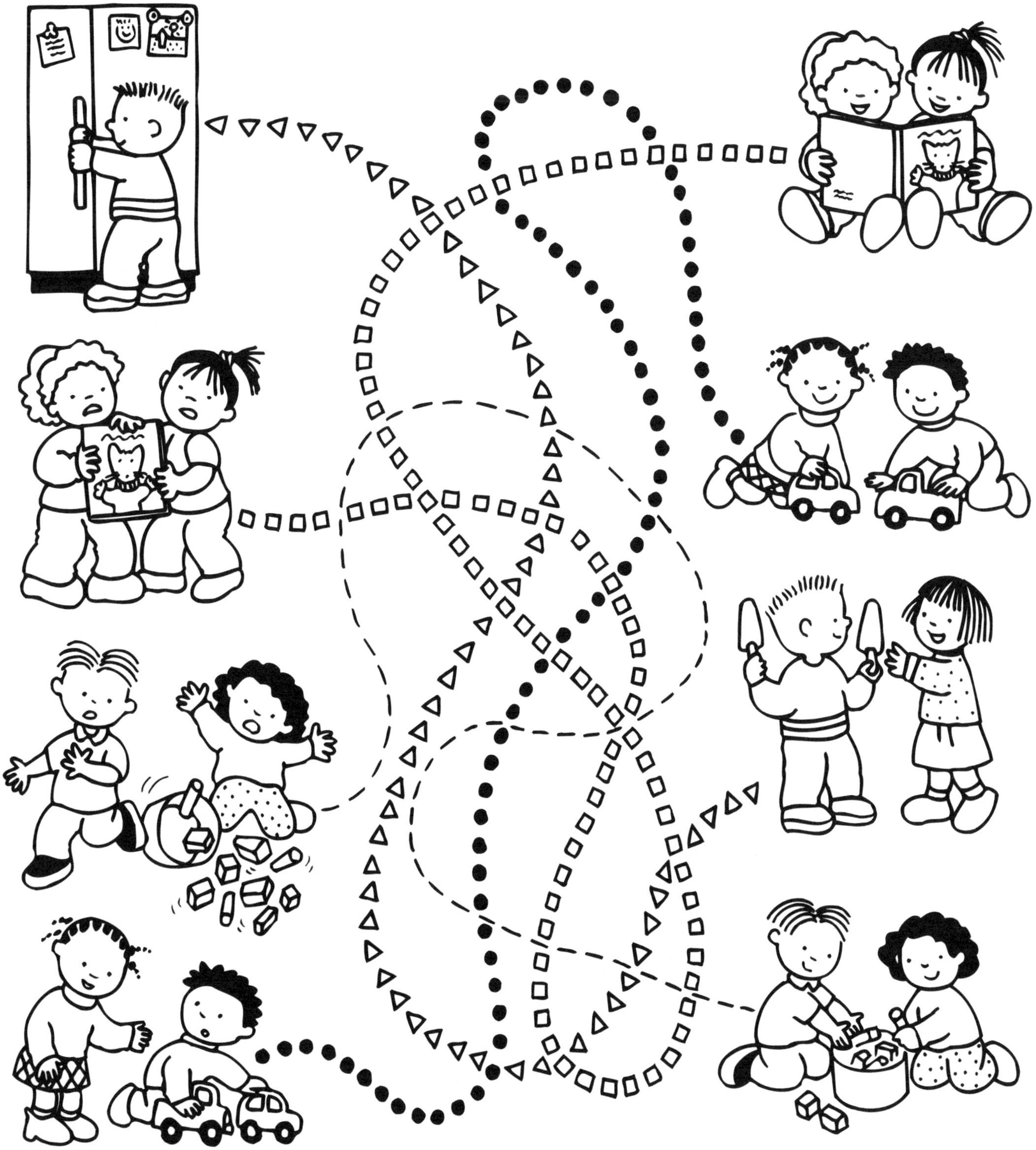

We can choose to show God's love.
Our Bible says, "Love your neighbor." Matthew 22:39

Draw a picture of a way you can show God's love to a friend.
Draw a path between you and your friend.

Find and draw a ○ around the numbers 1 to 10 hidden in the picture.

1	2	3	4	5	6	7	8	9	10

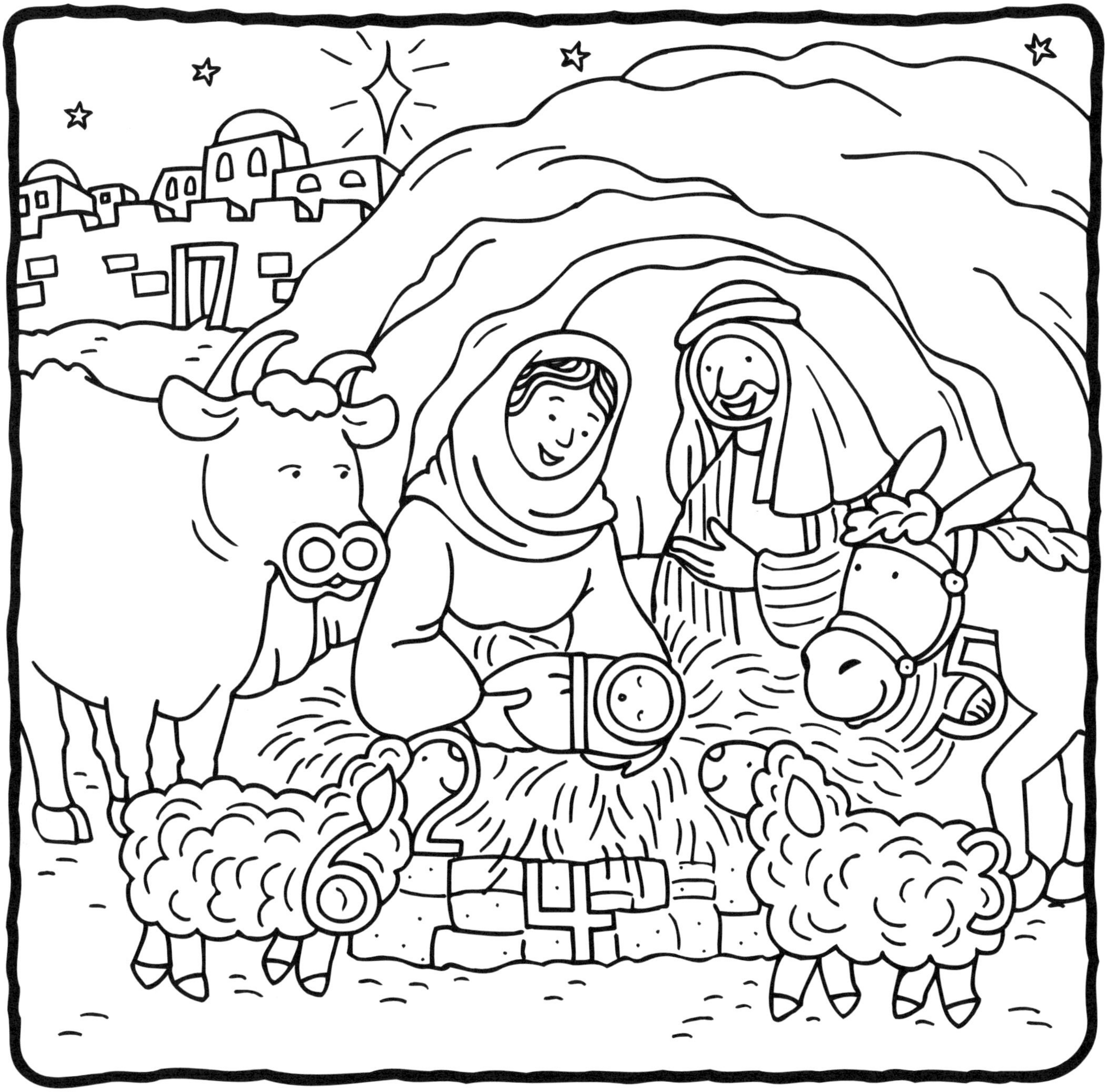

We are glad that Jesus is born!
Our Bible says, "God's Son is born for us." (See Isaiah 9:6.)

As you point to each number you found, hold up that number of fingers.

Draw a ○ around the manger in the box that matches the one the children are playing with. Then do the same with the cow.

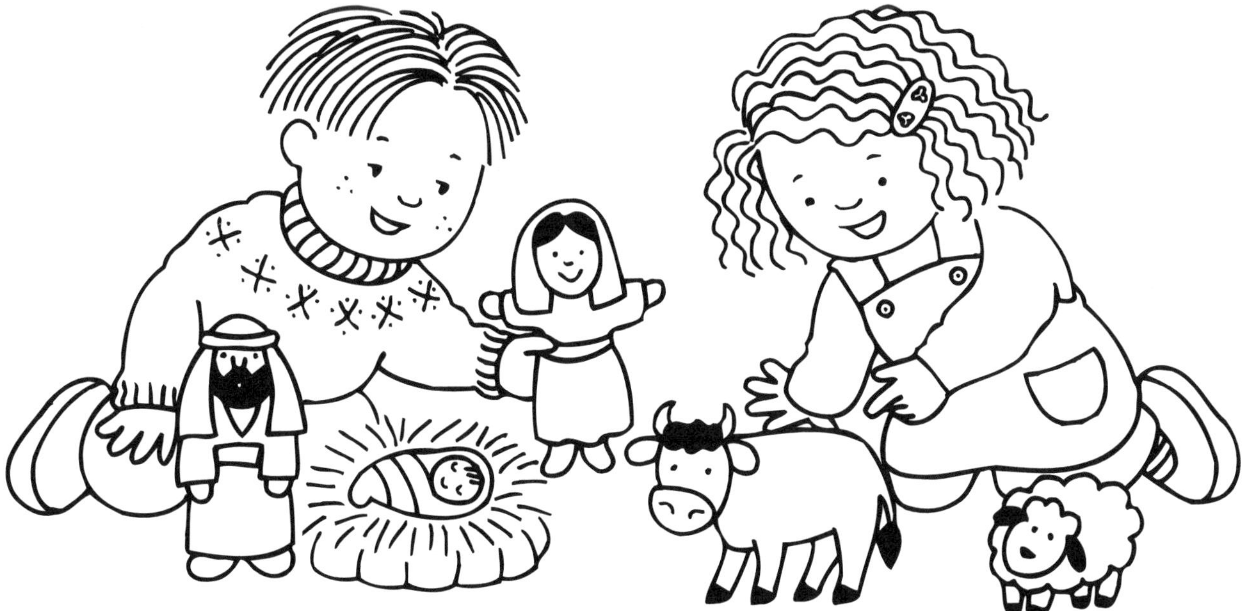

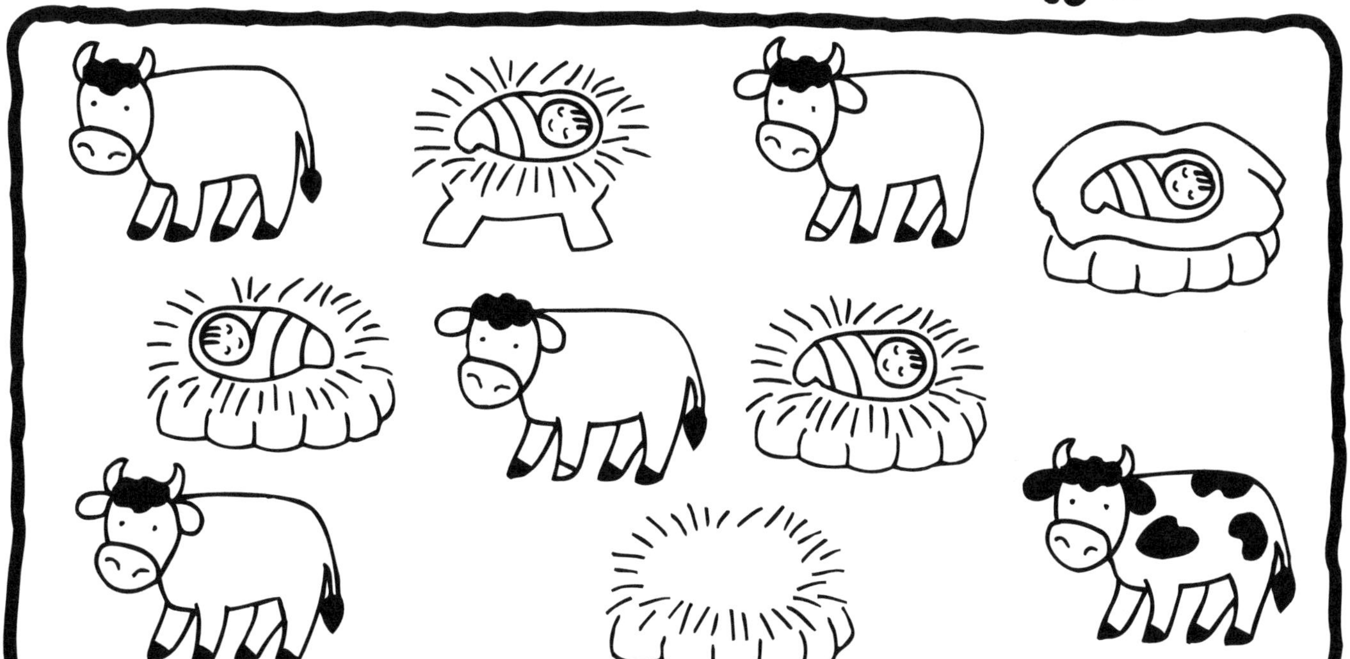

God sent Jesus to be born. We are glad!
Our Bible says, "God's Son is born for us." (See Isaiah 9:6.)

Color the matching figures to look the same.

Complete the dot-to-dots to see who came to visit baby Jesus.

The shepherds told people the good news that Jesus was born.
We can tell people the good news, too.
Our Bible says, "Good news! Today Jesus has been born." (See Luke 2:10-11.)

Cross off all the numbers below.
Have someone help you read the words that are left. Say the good news together!

1	2	J	3	e	4	5	s	u	s	6	i	7	s	8	9	b	5	o	2	3	r	n	4

Look at these pictures of people celebrating the good news that Jesus is born.
In each picture, draw a ○ around the person who is the shortest.

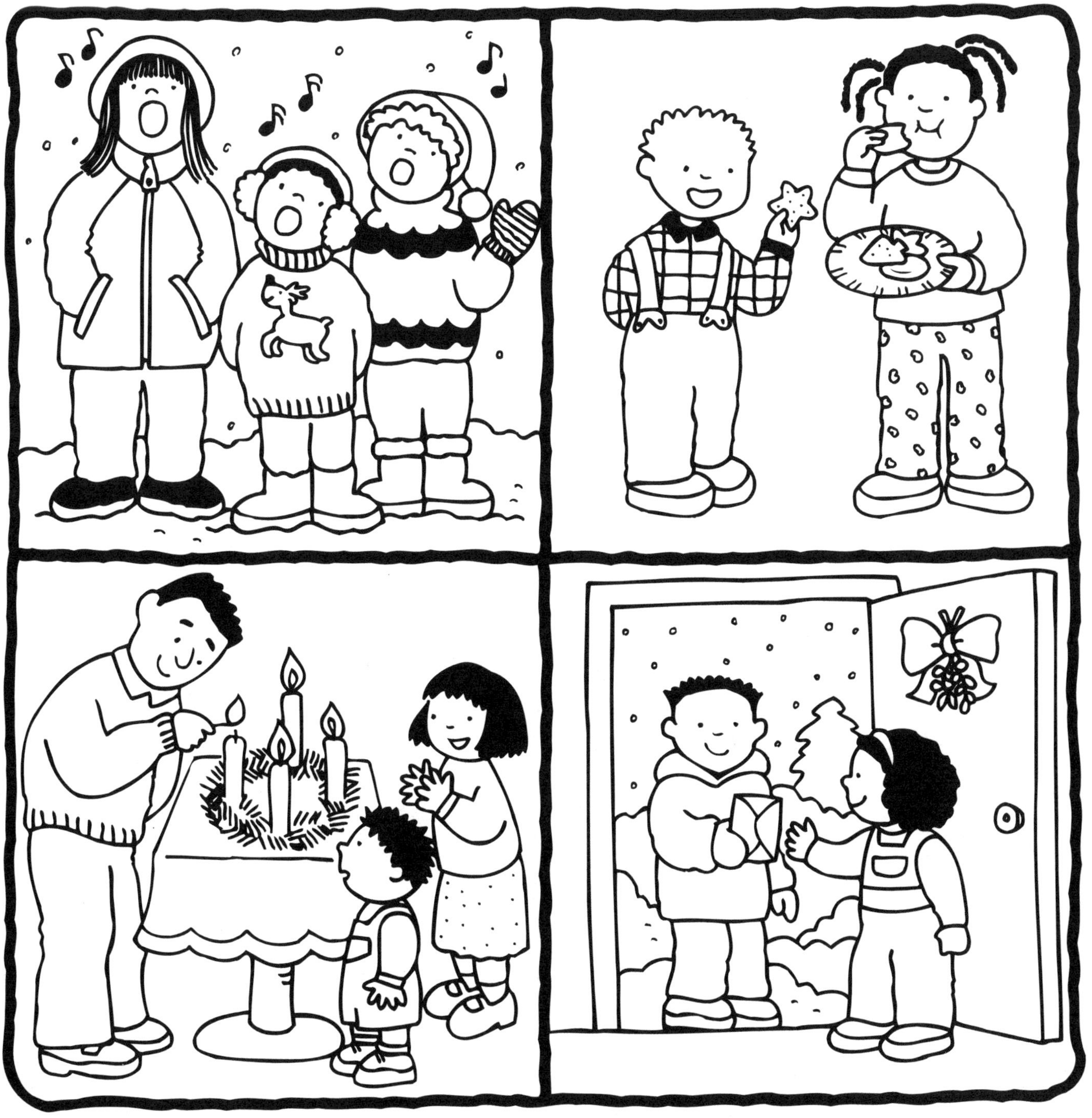

We can tell others the good news that Jesus is born.
Our Bible says, "Good news! Today Jesus has been born." (See Luke 2:10-11.)

Draw a picture of your favorite way to celebrate the good news that Jesus is born. Tell someone about your picture!

Trace the path Joseph, Mary and Jesus should take to get to Egypt.

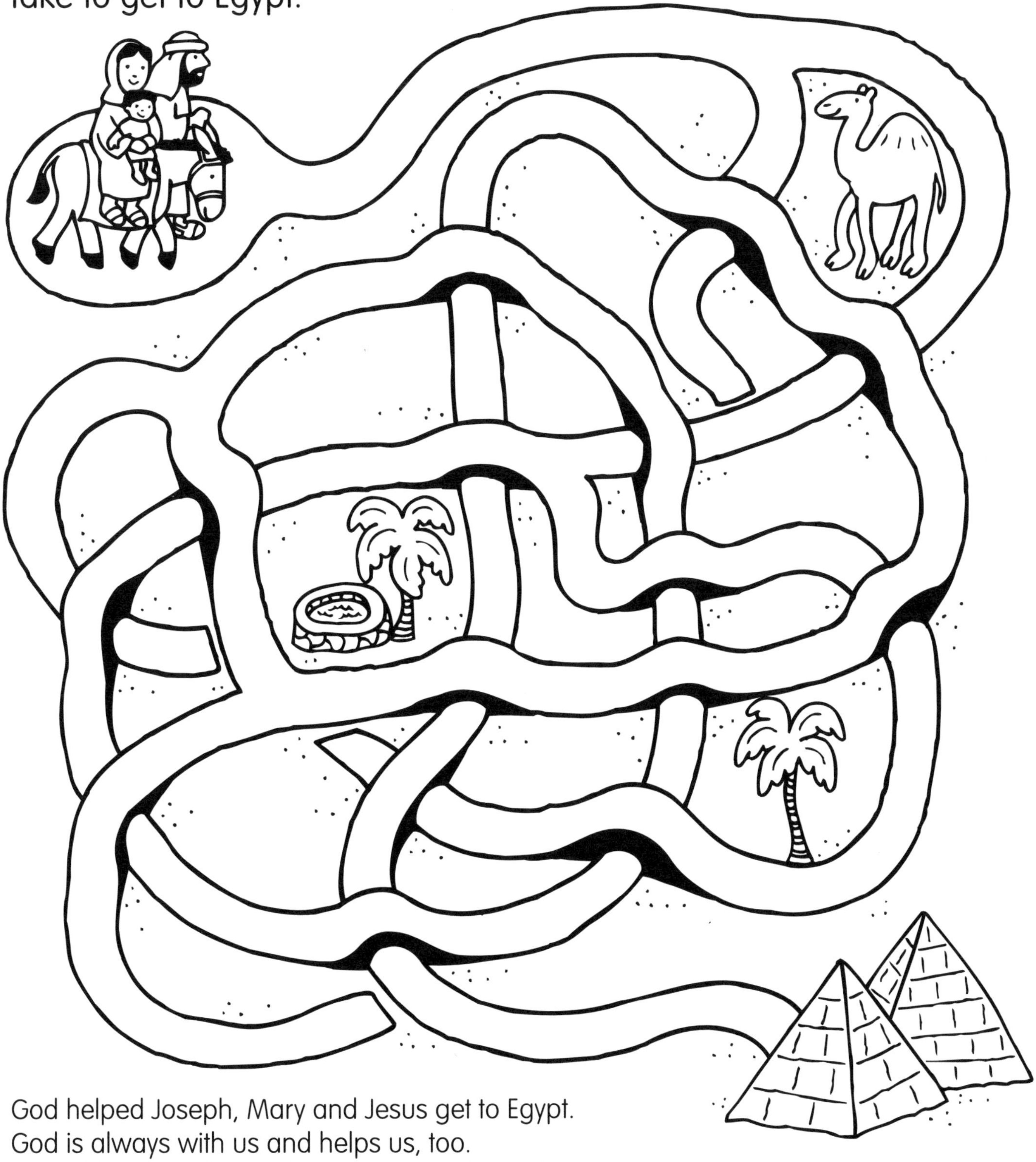

God helped Joseph, Mary and Jesus get to Egypt.
God is always with us and helps us, too.
Our Bible says, "The Lord your God is with you." Zephaniah 3:17

Draw a picture of how you would like to travel if you were taking a trip.

Where are these children?
Draw lines to match the children who are in the same place.

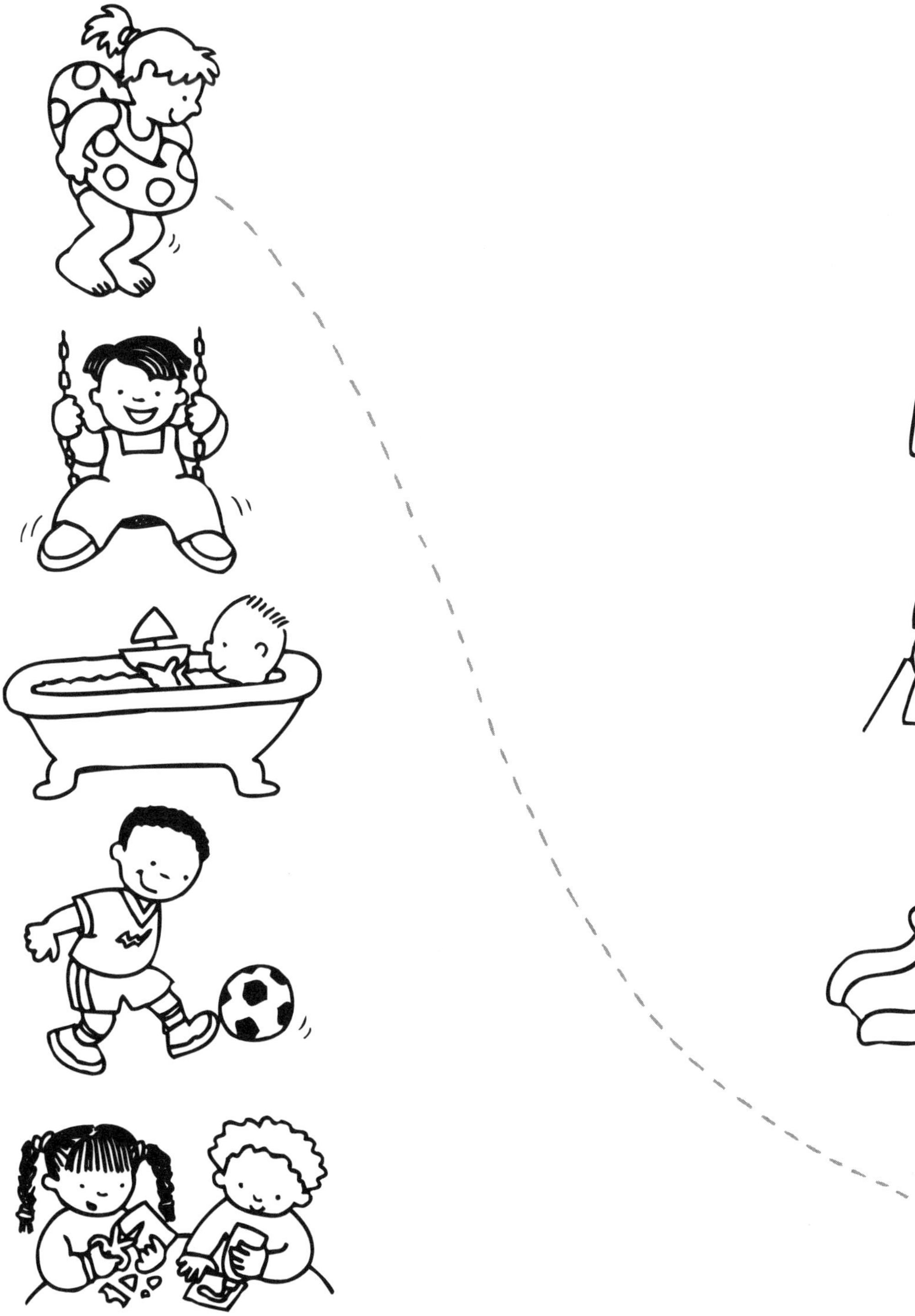

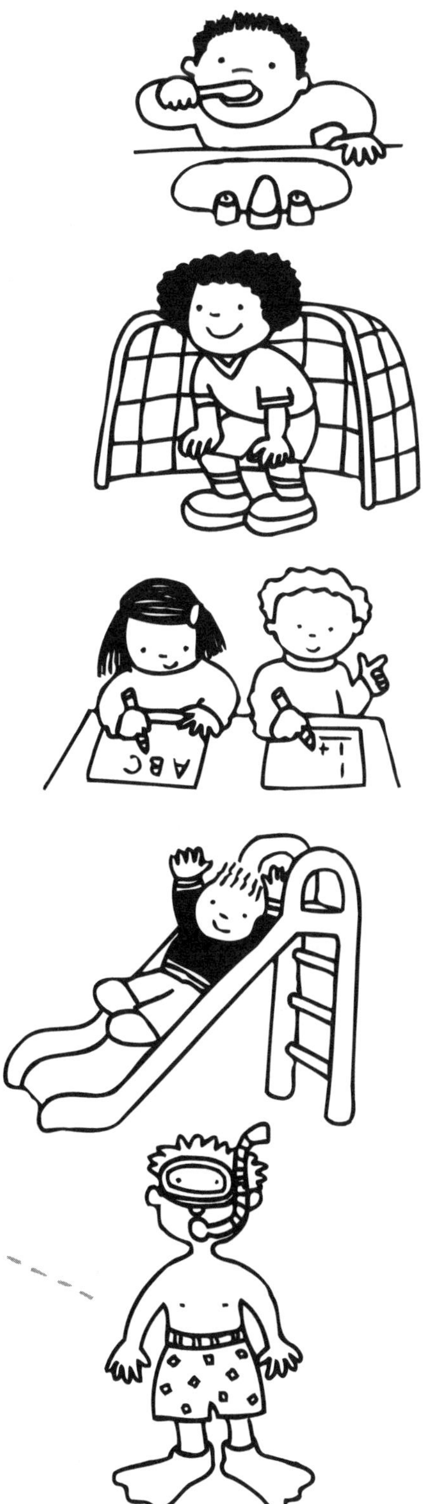

God is with us wherever we go.
Our Bible says, "The Lord your God is with you." Zephaniah 3:17

Draw a ◯ around your 3 favorite activities.
Then draw a picture of yourself doing 1 of those activities.

What a crowd at the Temple!
Draw a line from Mary and Joseph to Jesus. 

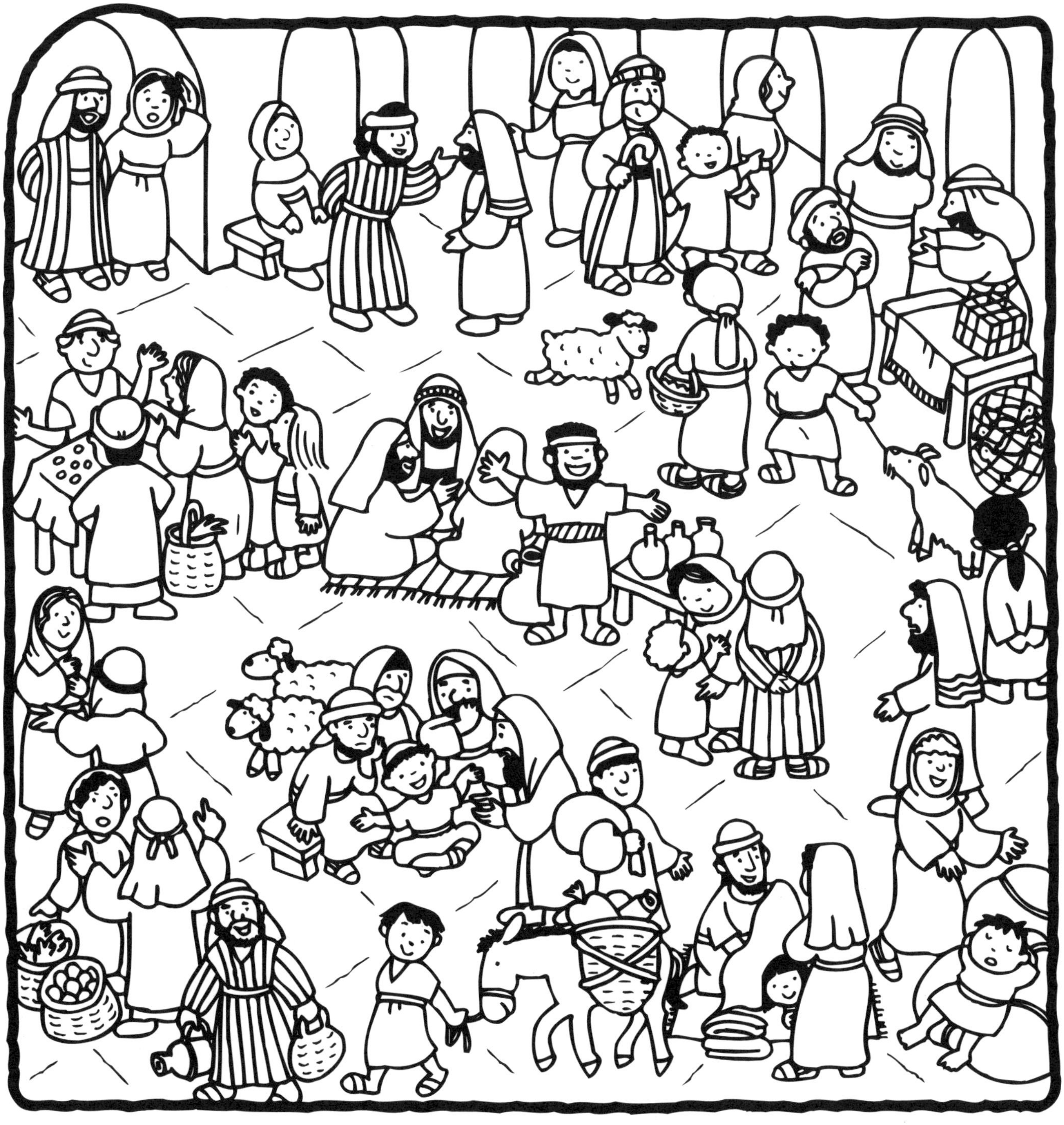

Mary and Joseph loved Jesus and helped Him as He grew.
God gives people to love and help us grow, too.
Our Bible says, "God's love for me is great." (See Psalm 86:13.)

How many men have striped robes? __________
How many men have something covering their hair? __________

Draw a ○ around the picture in each row that is different.

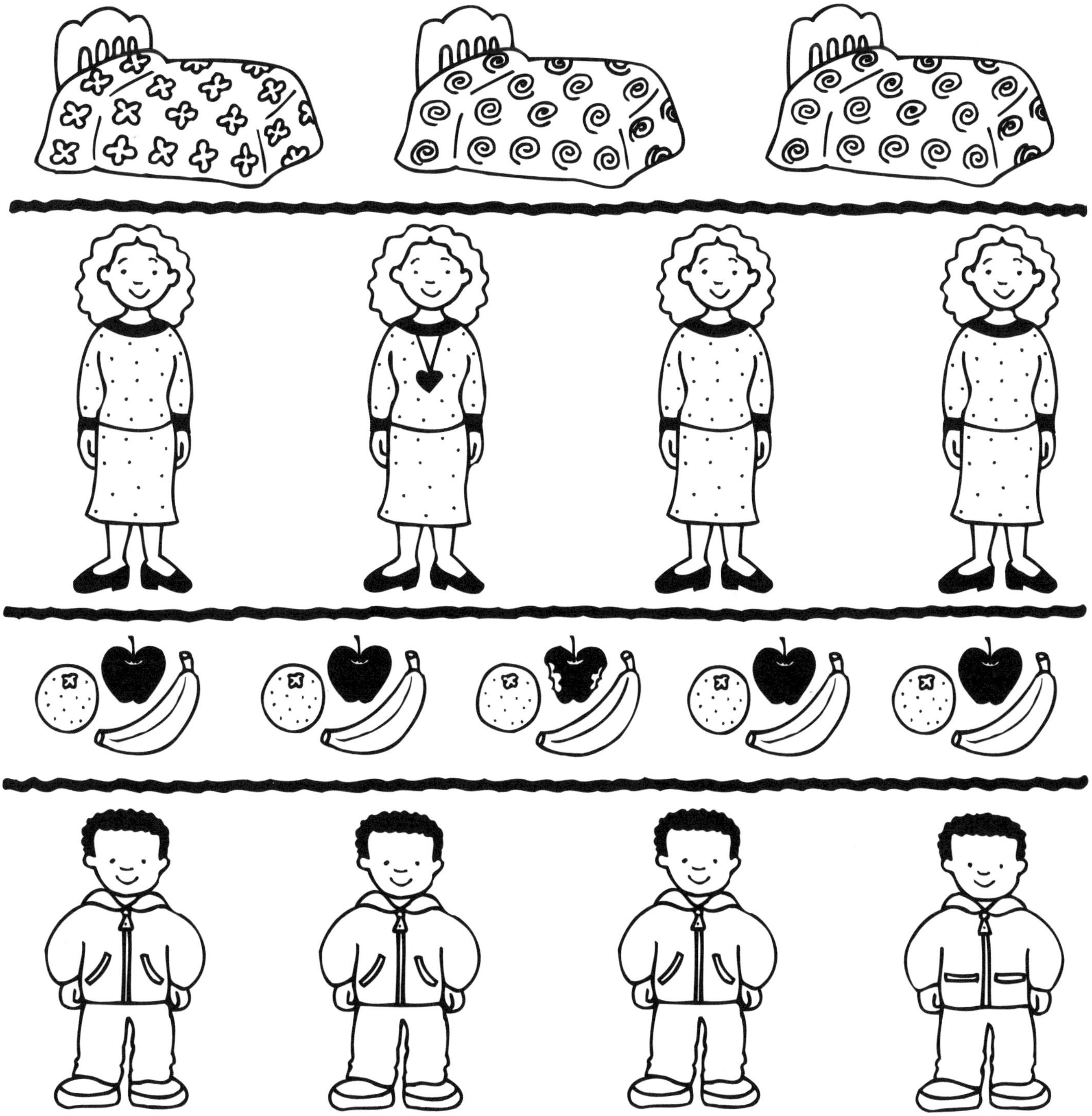

God loves and gives us what we need as we grow.
We can thank God for His great love for us.
Our Bible says, "God's love for me is great." (See Psalm 86:13.)

Color the pictures in each row to make each picture different.

In this picture of the angel talking to Zechariah,
how many ○s can you find? ________
How many □s? ________
How many ▭s? ________
How many △s? ________

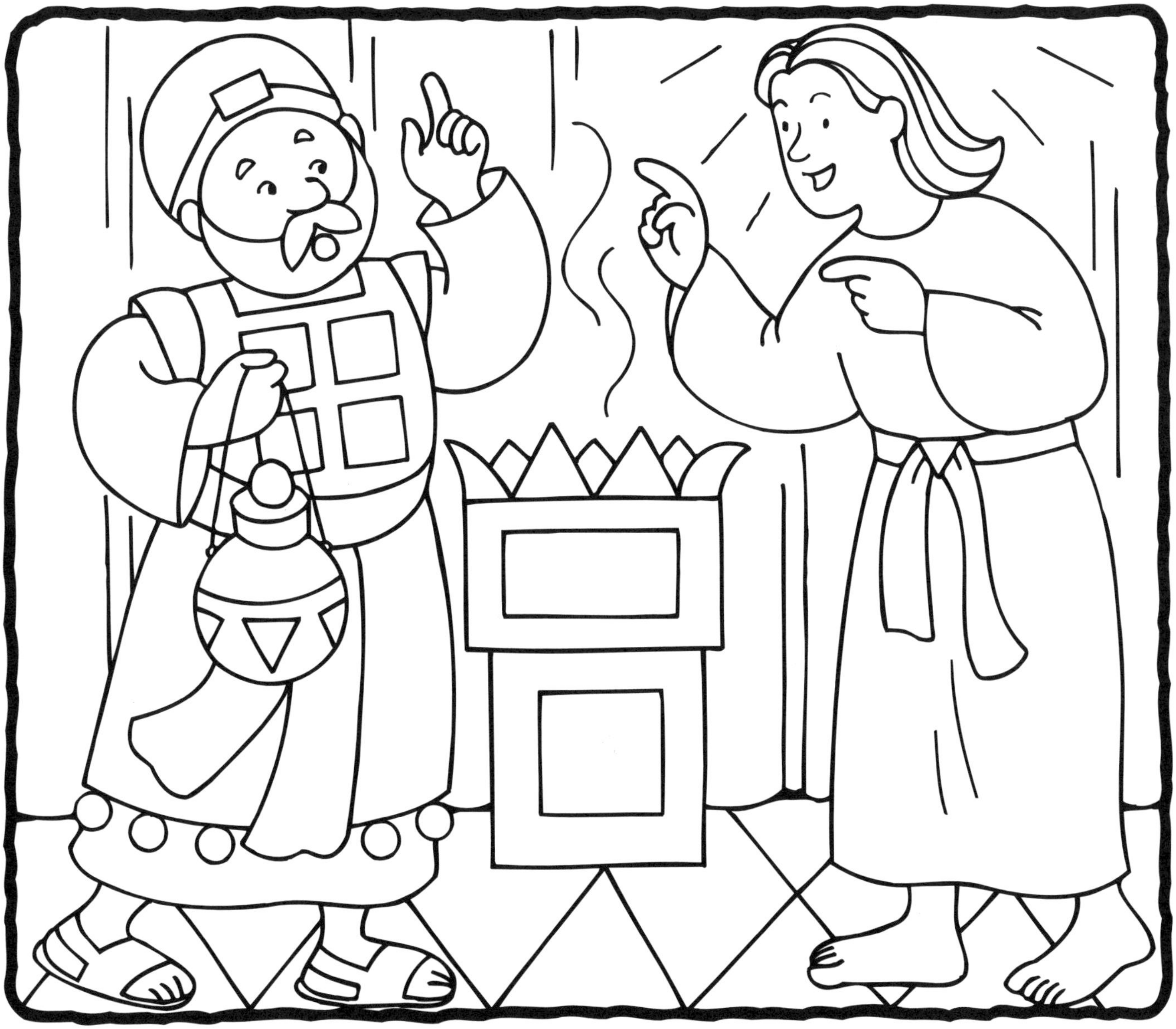

The angel told Zechariah he would have a son named John.
John would tell the good news that Jesus is God's Son.
Our Bible says, "God so loved the world that he gave his one and only Son." John 3:16

Write a **c** on each ○. Write an **s** on each □.
Write an **r** on each ▭. Write a **t** on each △.

Draw lines to show where each child lives.

God loves all people, no matter where they live or what they like to play.
God sent Jesus to show His love for all people.
Our Bible says, "God so loved the world that he gave his one and only Son." John 3:16

Color the object each child is holding.
What does each child like to do?

Draw lines to show where these faces are in the picture below.

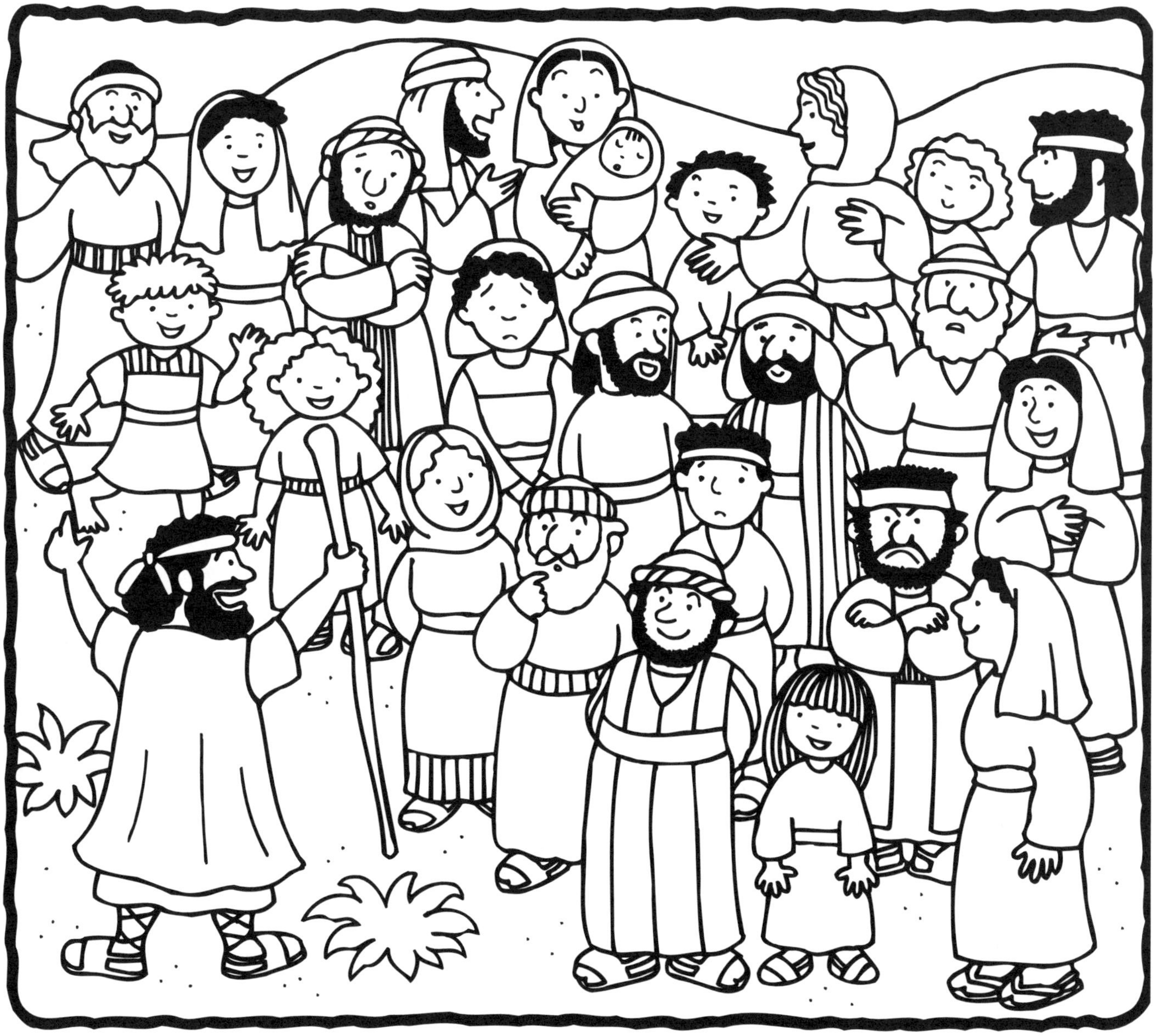

John told people to do good.
Jesus helps us do good.
Our Bible says, "Stop doing wrong and do good." (See Psalm 34:14.)

Color a person who looks happy YELLOW.
Color a person who looks angry RED.
Color a person who looks sad BLUE.

Color the △s in the path to find something good to do.

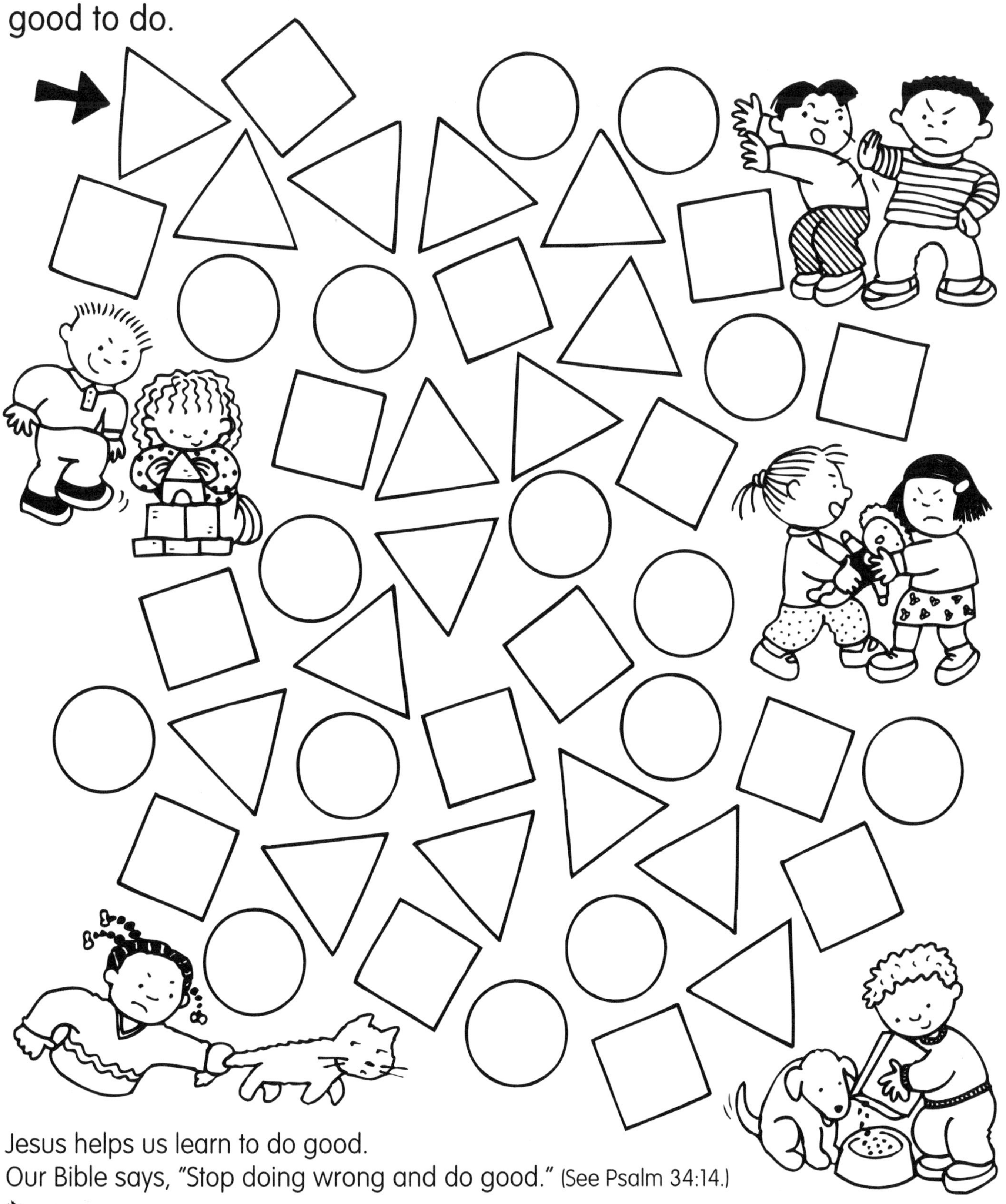

Jesus helps us learn to do good.
Our Bible says, "Stop doing wrong and do good." (See Psalm 34:14.)

Draw something good that Jesus can help you do.
Then draw a big ○ around your picture.

In the picture, find and draw a ○ around the letters of Jesus' name.

J E S U S

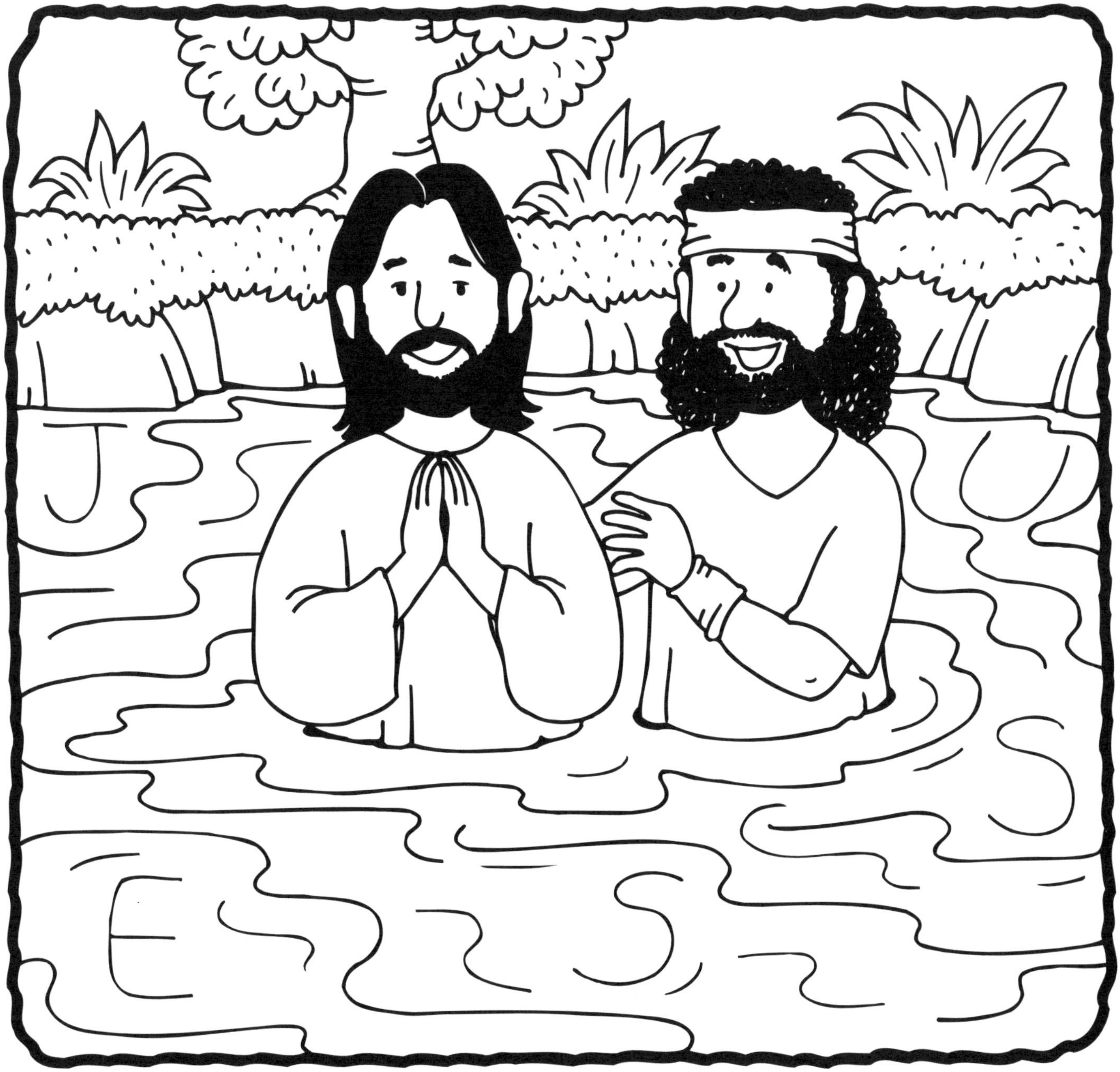

John baptized Jesus, God's Son.
We are glad God sent His Son, Jesus.
Our Bible says, "Jesus is the Son of God." (See John 1:34.)

How many letters are in Jesus' name? _______
Draw that number of fish in the river.

On the picnic blanket, draw a ○ around what belongs to the boy.
Draw a □ around what belongs to the girl .

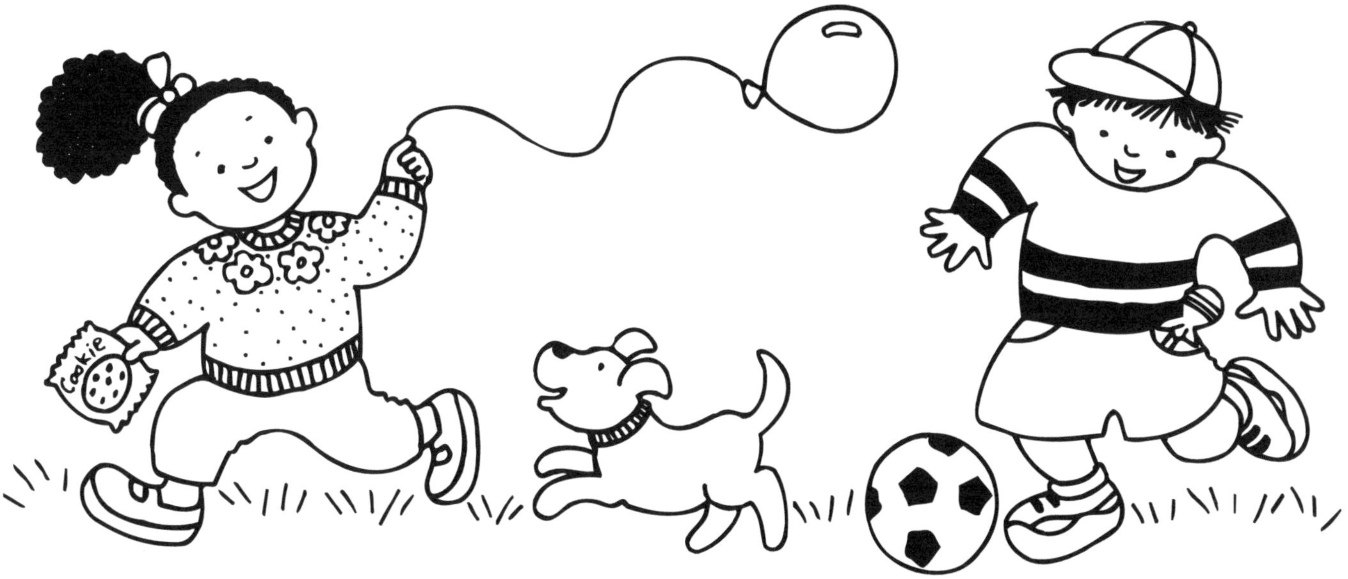

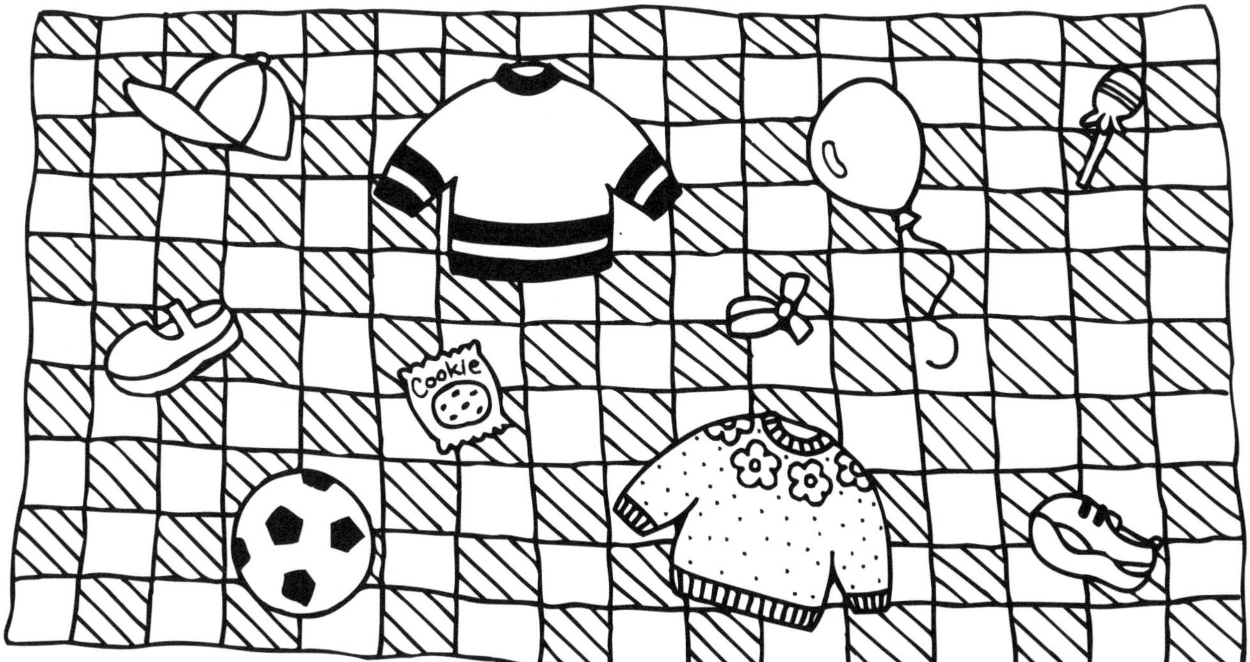

These children are glad!
We show we're glad in many ways.
We are glad that God sent His Son, Jesus.
Our Bible says, "Jesus is the Son of God." (See John 1:34.)

Draw a picture of how you look when you are glad.

In each picture, Jesus' helpers are following Him.
Are they walking left or right?
Draw a ○ around the correct word under each picture.

← left right →

Jesus' helpers followed Him.
They learned about Jesus and God's love.
We can learn about Jesus and God's love, too.
Our Bible tells us, "'Come, follow me,' Jesus said." Matthew 4:19

Draw a picture of yourself following Jesus.
Are you facing left or right? Write **left** or **right** under your picture.

Trace each path to find a way to learn about Jesus.
You can use a different color to trace each path.

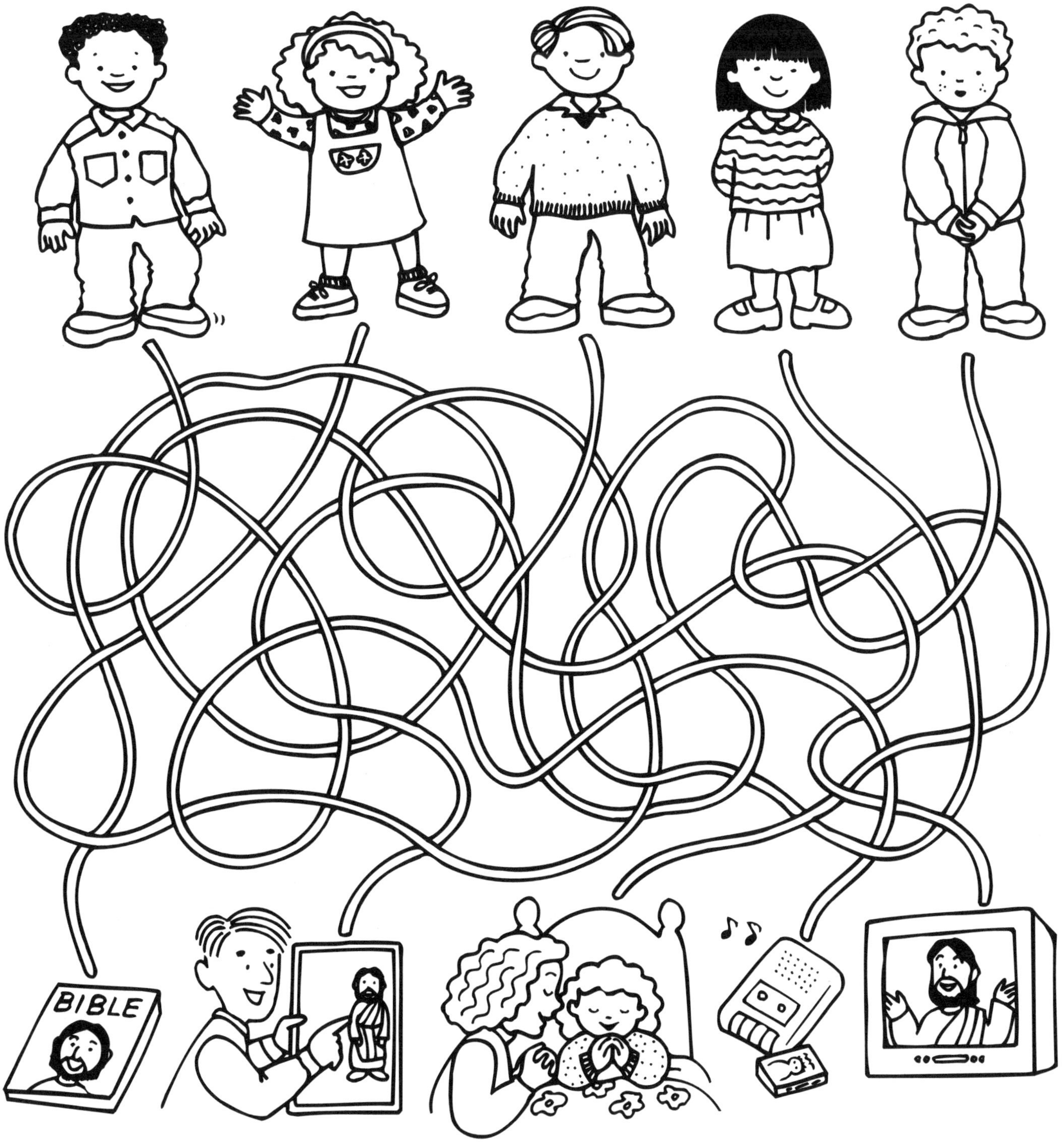

We can learn about Jesus and His love.
Our Bible tells us, "'Come, follow me,' Jesus said." Matthew 4:19

Trace the letters to spell Jesus' name.
Draw a O around His name in 2 other places on this page.

Count each set of objects and write the number.

In each row, draw a ◯ around the set that has **more** than the others.

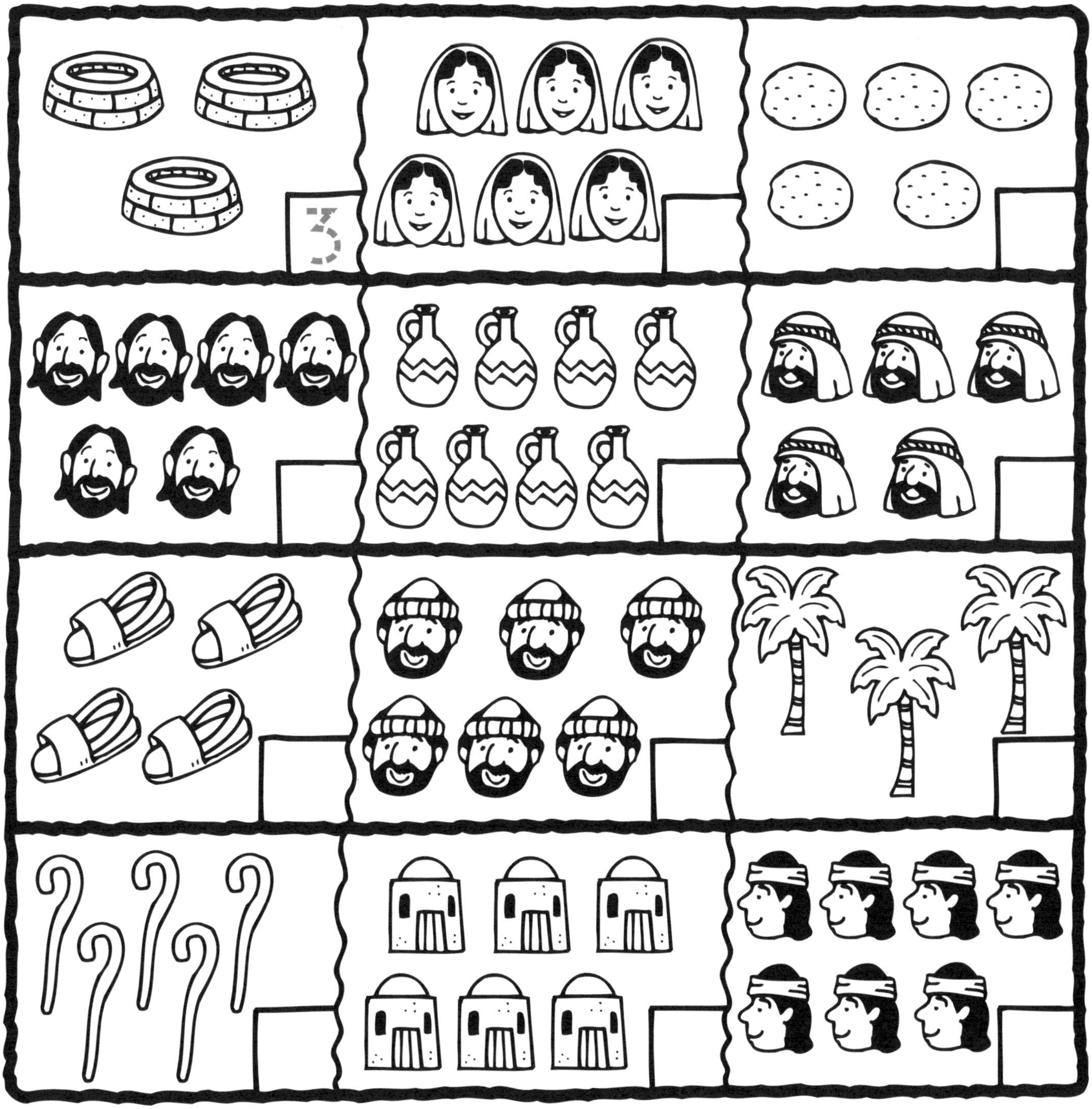

3

The woman at the well was glad that Jesus loved her.
Jesus loves us, too!
Our Bible says, "I will be glad and rejoice in your love." Psalm 31:7

In each row, draw an ✖ on some objects so that all sets in that row have the same number of objects.

Draw an ✖ on every **c, e, f, h** and **k.**

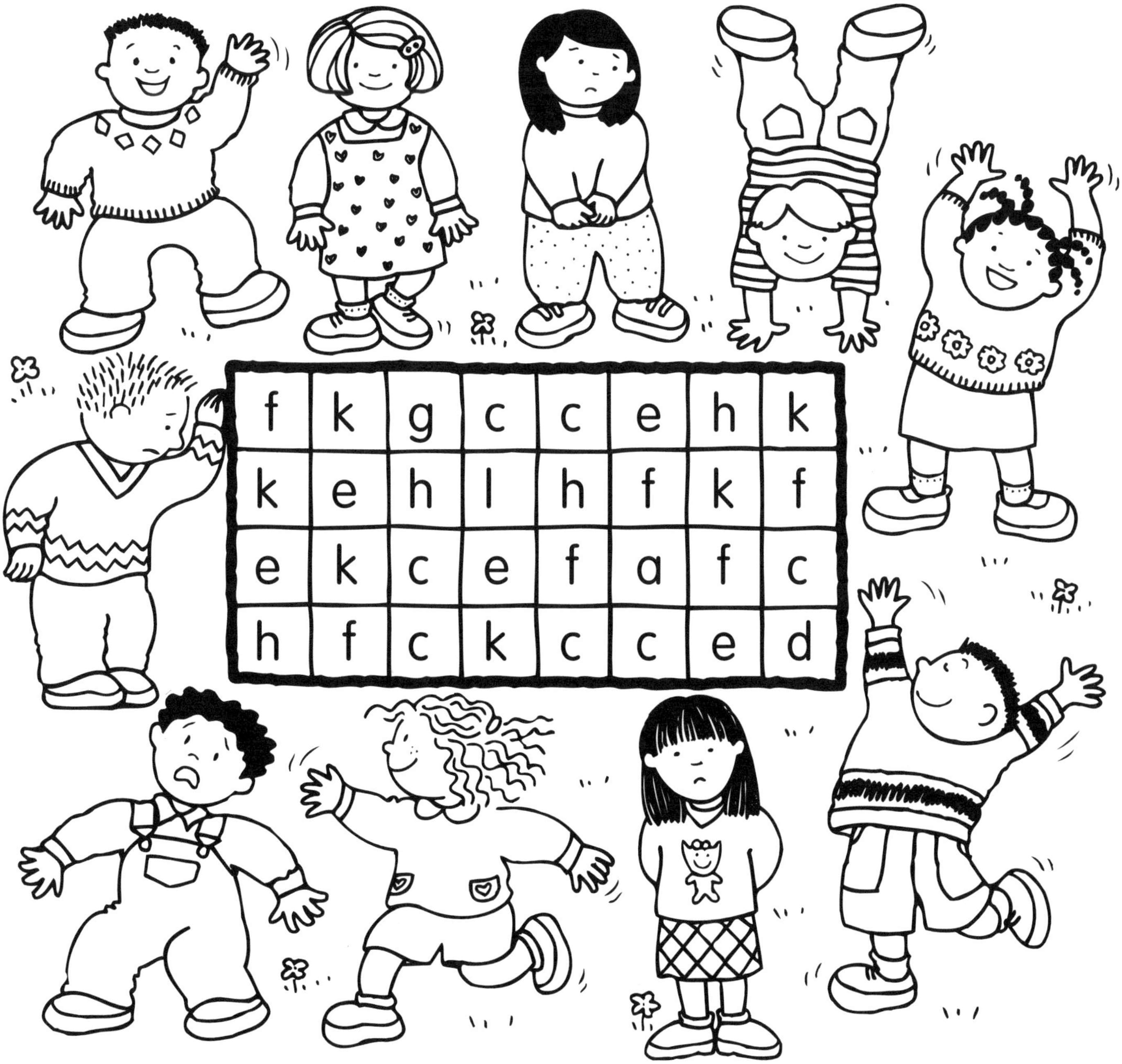

f	k	g	c	c	e	h	k
k	e	h	l	h	f	k	f
e	k	c	e	f	a	f	c
h	f	c	k	c	c	e	d

Write the leftover letters in order on the lines to spell the secret word.

_____ _____ _____ _____

We are glad that Jesus loves us!
Our Bible says, "I will be glad and rejoice in your love." Psalm 31:7

Color the children who look like they are glad.

Draw an ✖ on the pictures that are not part of the big picture.

Color in the little pictures that are part of the big picture.

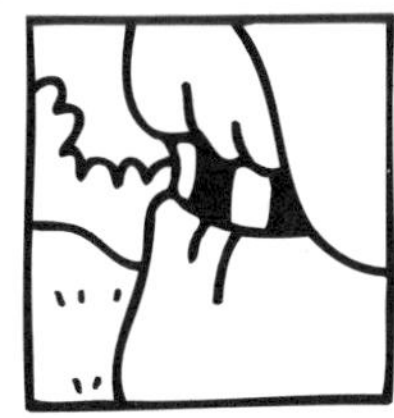

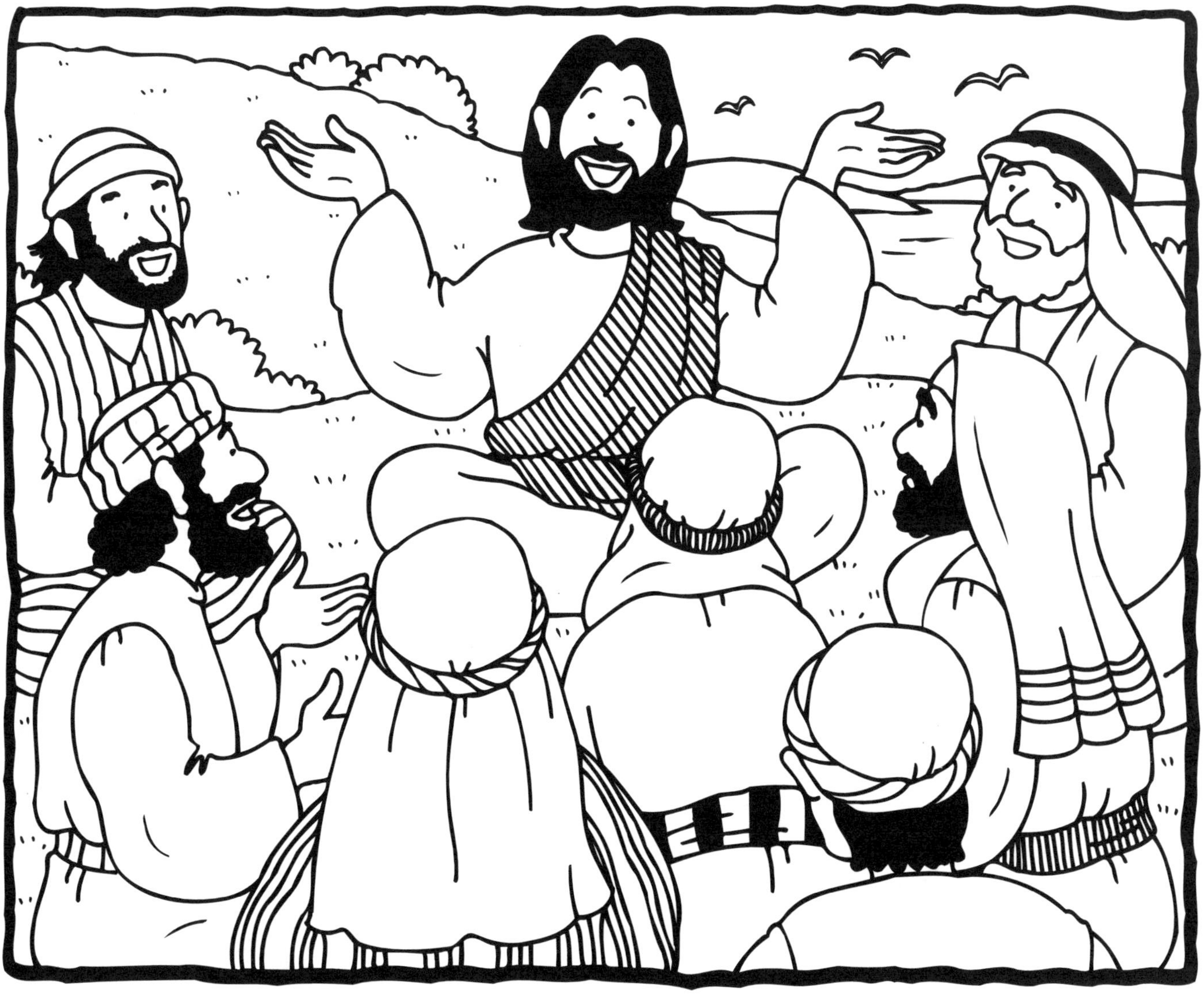

Jesus taught His helpers to pray to God.
We can pray to God, too. We can tell God we love Him.
Our Bible says, "Pray to God, and he will hear you." (See Job 22:27.)

Draw a picture of yourself praying.
Hide the letters **P, R, A** and **Y** in the picture.
Give your picture to a friend, so your friend can find the hidden letters in it.

These children are holding things they want to thank God for.
The name of each child has the same beginning sound as the object he or she is holding.
Draw a line to match each child with his or her name.

Jack
Carlee
Sam
Anna
Ben

When we pray to God, we can tell Him we love Him.
We can thank Him for everything He has given us.
Our Bible says, "Pray to God, and he will hear you." (See Job 22:27.)

Draw a picture of yourself holding something that has the same beginning sound as your name.
Thank God for what you are holding.

Color in all the spaces with children in them.

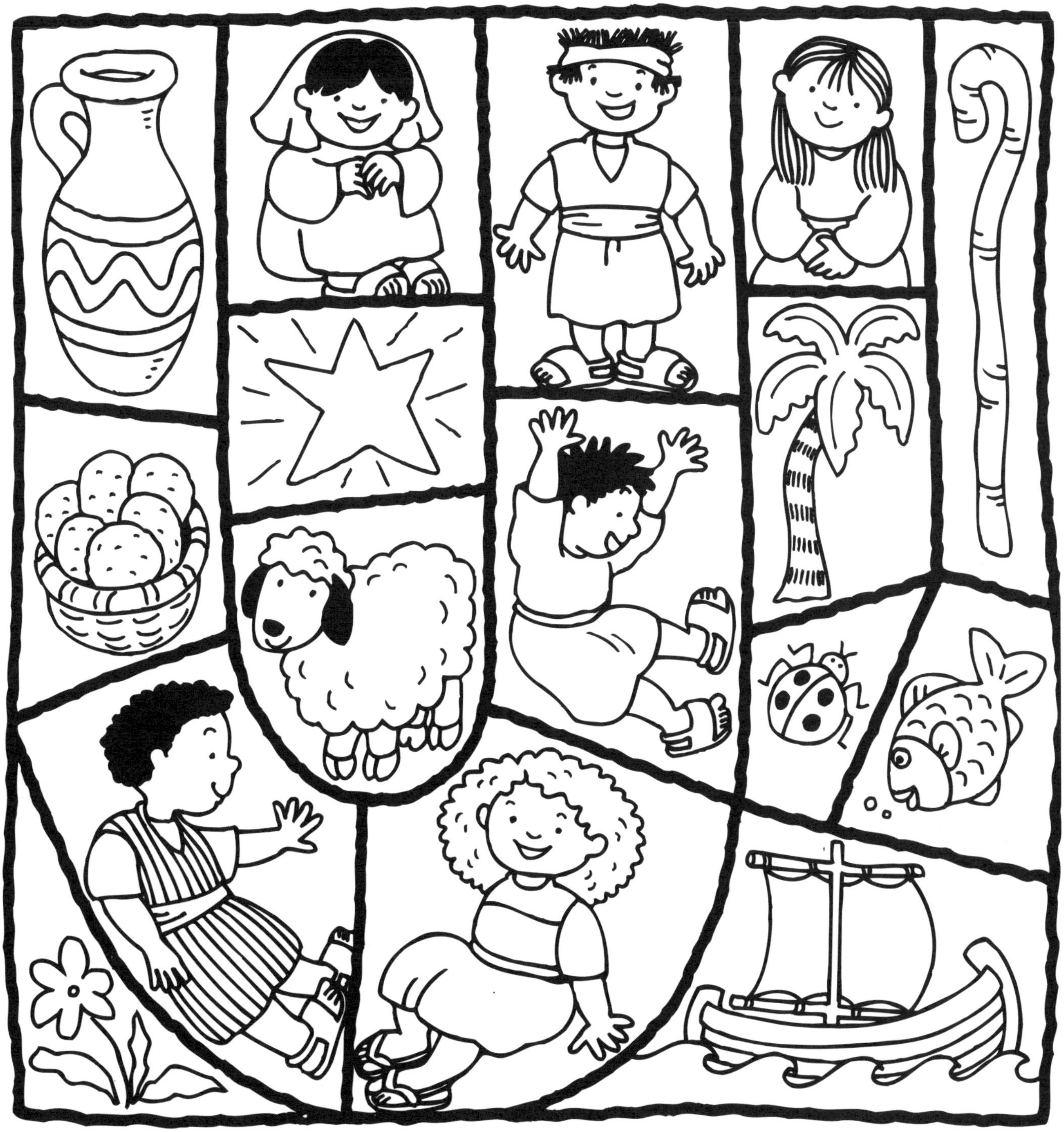

What letter did you make? J is the first letter in Jesus' name.
Jesus loves and cares for you!
Our Bible tells us, "Jesus said, 'Let the little children come to me.'" Matthew 19:14

Write your name. Are any letters the same as in Jesus' name?
Practice writing Jesus' name. He loves you!

Draw a ○ around the first child in each line.
Draw a □ around the last child in each line.

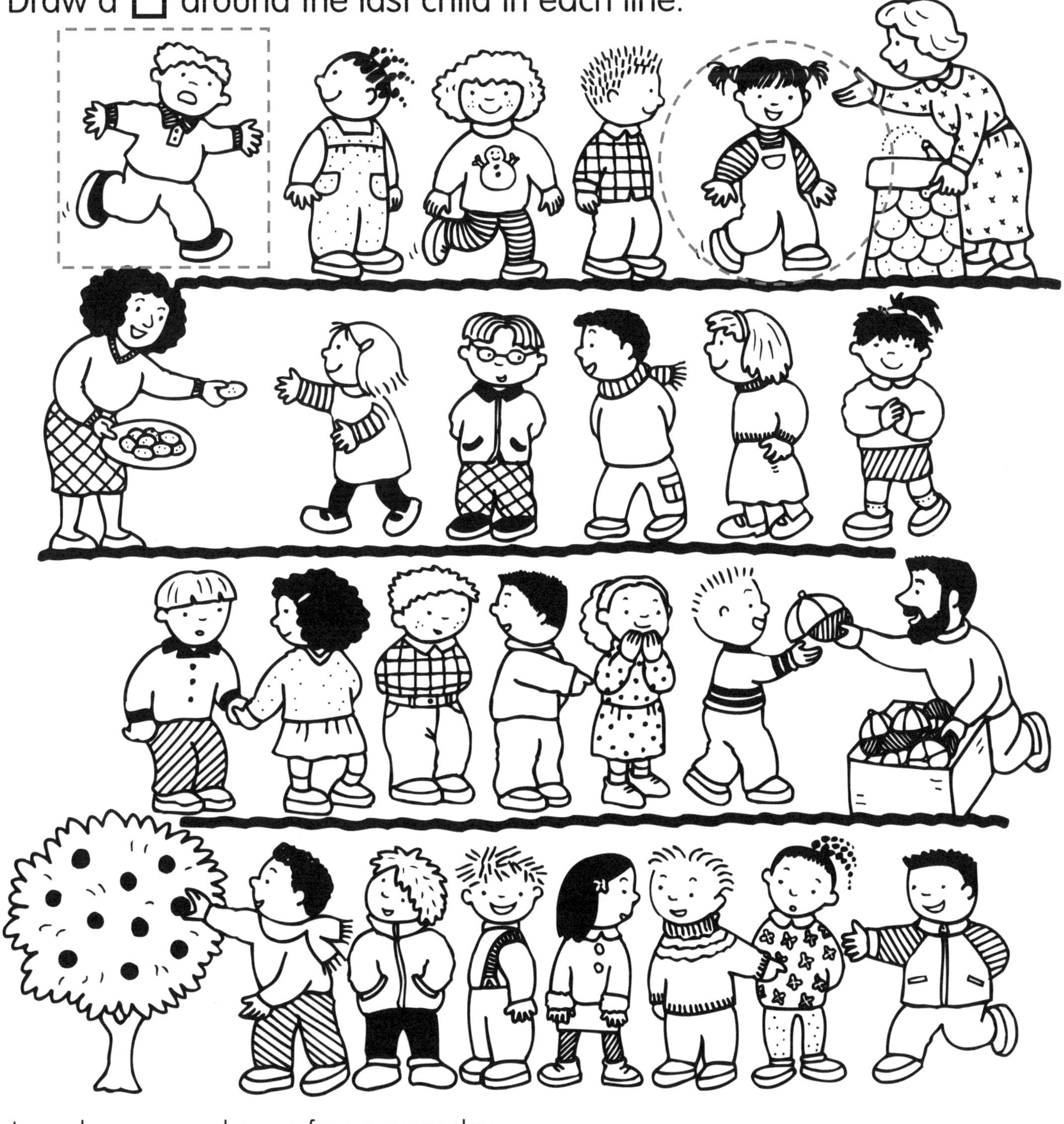

Jesus loves us and cares for us every day.
Jesus gives us people to love us, food to eat and clothes to wear.
Our Bible tells us, "Jesus said, 'Let the little children come to me.'" Matthew 19:14

Draw a ★ by the things on this page that remind you of Jesus' love for you.

Follow the maze through the tree.

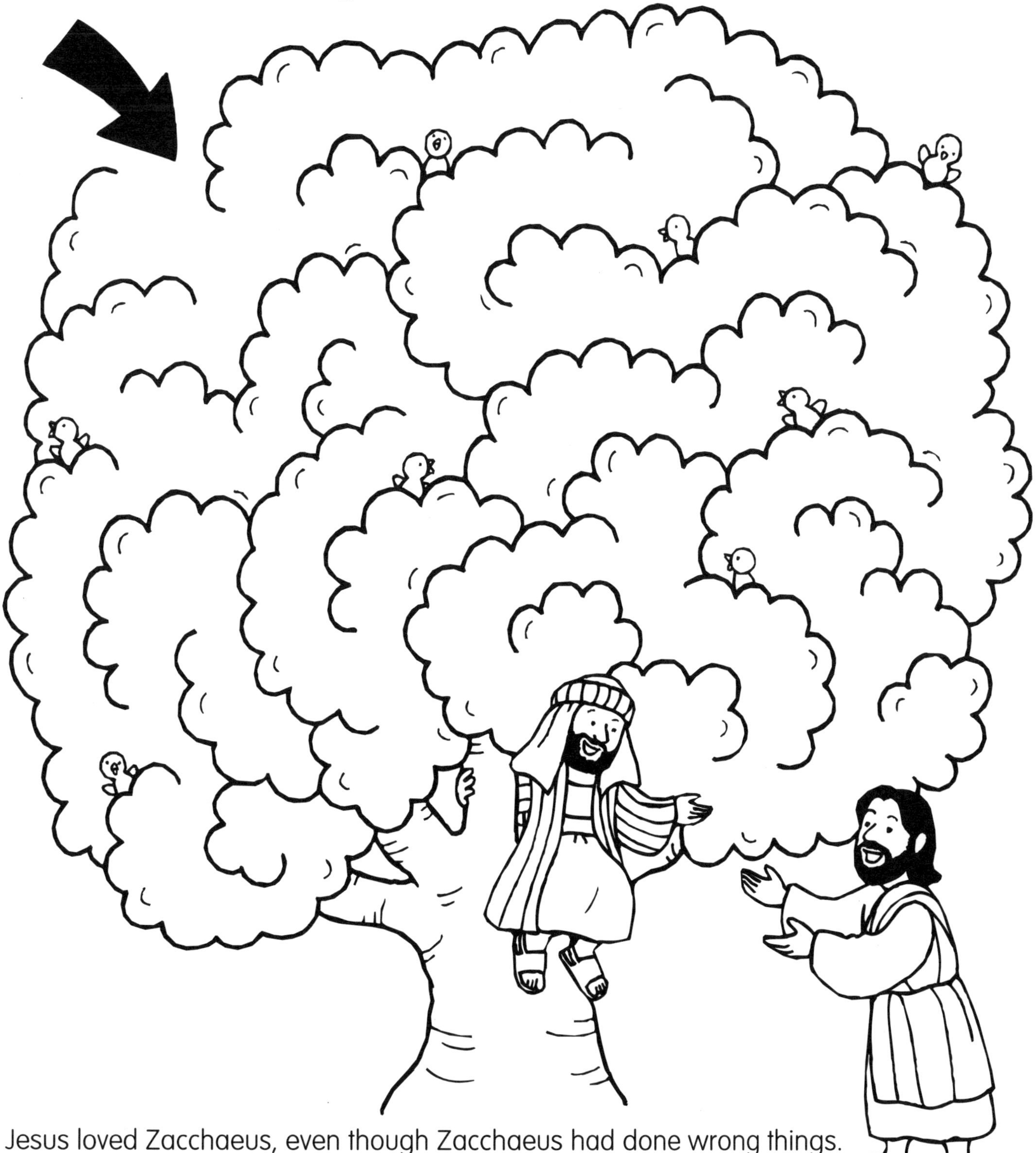

Jesus loved Zacchaeus, even though Zacchaeus had done wrong things.
Jesus loves us, too, even when we do wrong.
Our Bible says, "You are kind and forgiving, O Lord." (See Psalm 86:5.)

Look for another way through the tree.

There are at least 10 differences between these 2 pictures. How many can you find?
Draw an ✖ on a number when you find a difference.

1	2	3	4	5	6	7	8	9	10	11	12	13	14	15

In the picture, draw an ✖ on the wrong thing the boys are doing.
Jesus loves us and forgives us, even when we do wrong.
Our Bible says, "You are kind and forgiving, O Lord." (See Psalm 86:5.)

Draw an ✖ on the uppercase letters to find what you can say to Jesus when you do something wrong.

H	p	R	l	e	T	a	s	e	Y	f	W	o	r	g	B	i	v	X	e	N	m	e

In each row, draw the coins that continue the pattern.

The poor woman gave all the coins she had to show her love to God.
We can show our love to God, too.
Our Bible says, "I love you, O Lord." Psalm 18:1

Design your own coin.

In each row, draw an ✖ on the child who is doing something different.

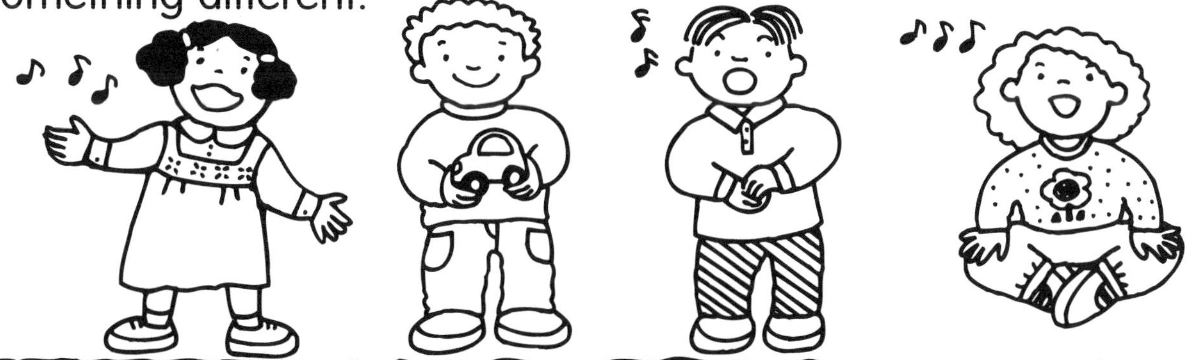

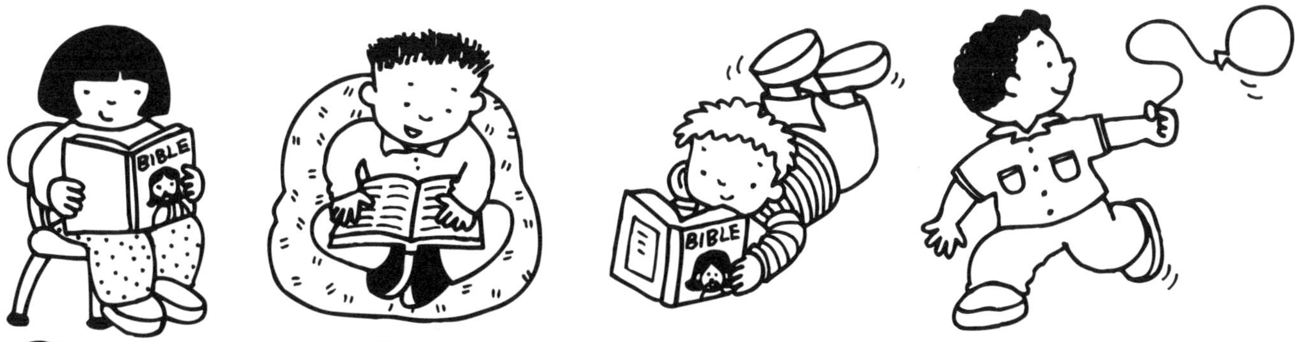

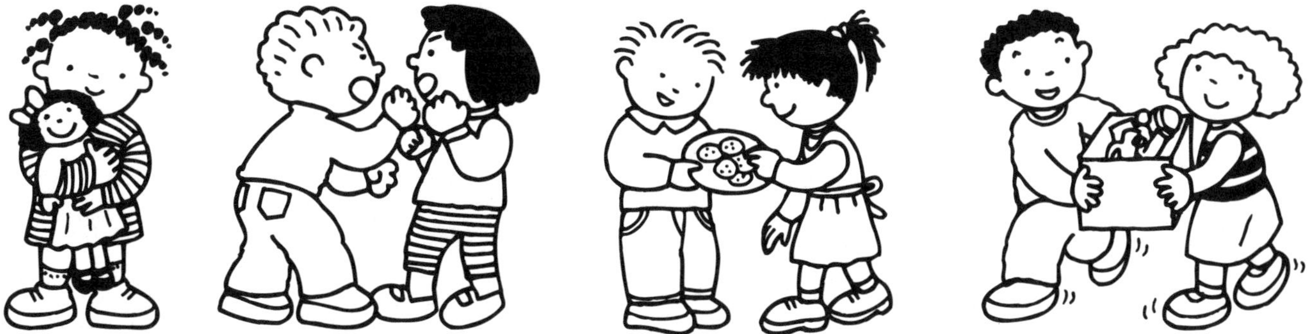

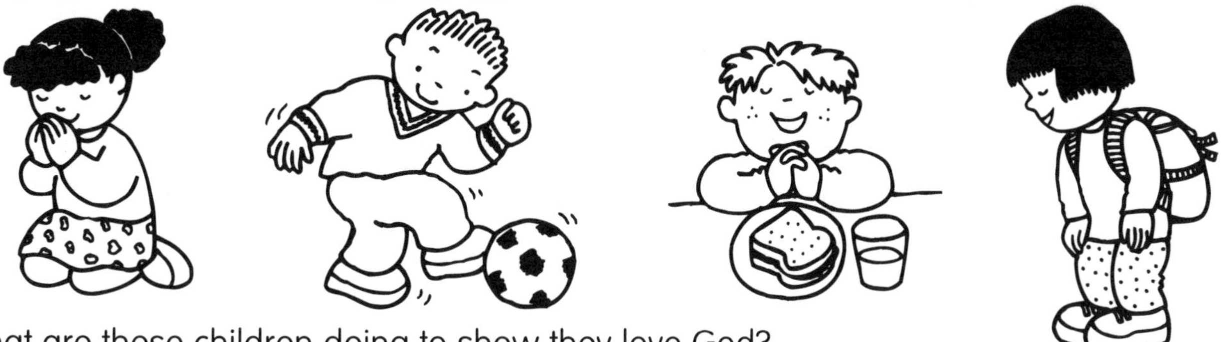

What are these children doing to show they love God?
We can show our love to God, too.
Our Bible says, "I love you, O Lord." Psalm 18:1

Color in the children showing ways you have shown your love to God.

A man asked Jesus to make his son well.
Help the man get back home to see his son.

Jesus loved the man and his son.
Jesus loves and teaches us about God's love, too.
Our Bible says, "Give thanks to the Lord. His love is forever." (See 1 Chronicles 16:34.)

The Bible says the son got better at the exact time Jesus said he would get better.
What time do these clocks show?

Draw a clock that shows 3:00.

Look at the numbers below the pictures in each row.
Draw a ○ around that many of each picture to make smaller sets.
Then count the items in each set to complete the number sentences.

1 + 3 + 2 = 6

1 3 2

3 + 3 =

3 3

5 + 2 =

5 2

2 + 4 + 3 =

2 4 3

Jesus loves all people.
Jesus loves us, too.
Our Bible says, "Give thanks to the Lord. His love is forever." (See 1 Chronicles 16:34.)

Draw 6 ☺s.
Draw 2 ○s around the ☺s to make a set of 2 and 4.
Write a number sentence about your ☺s.

Draw a ○ around the picture in each row that has something missing.

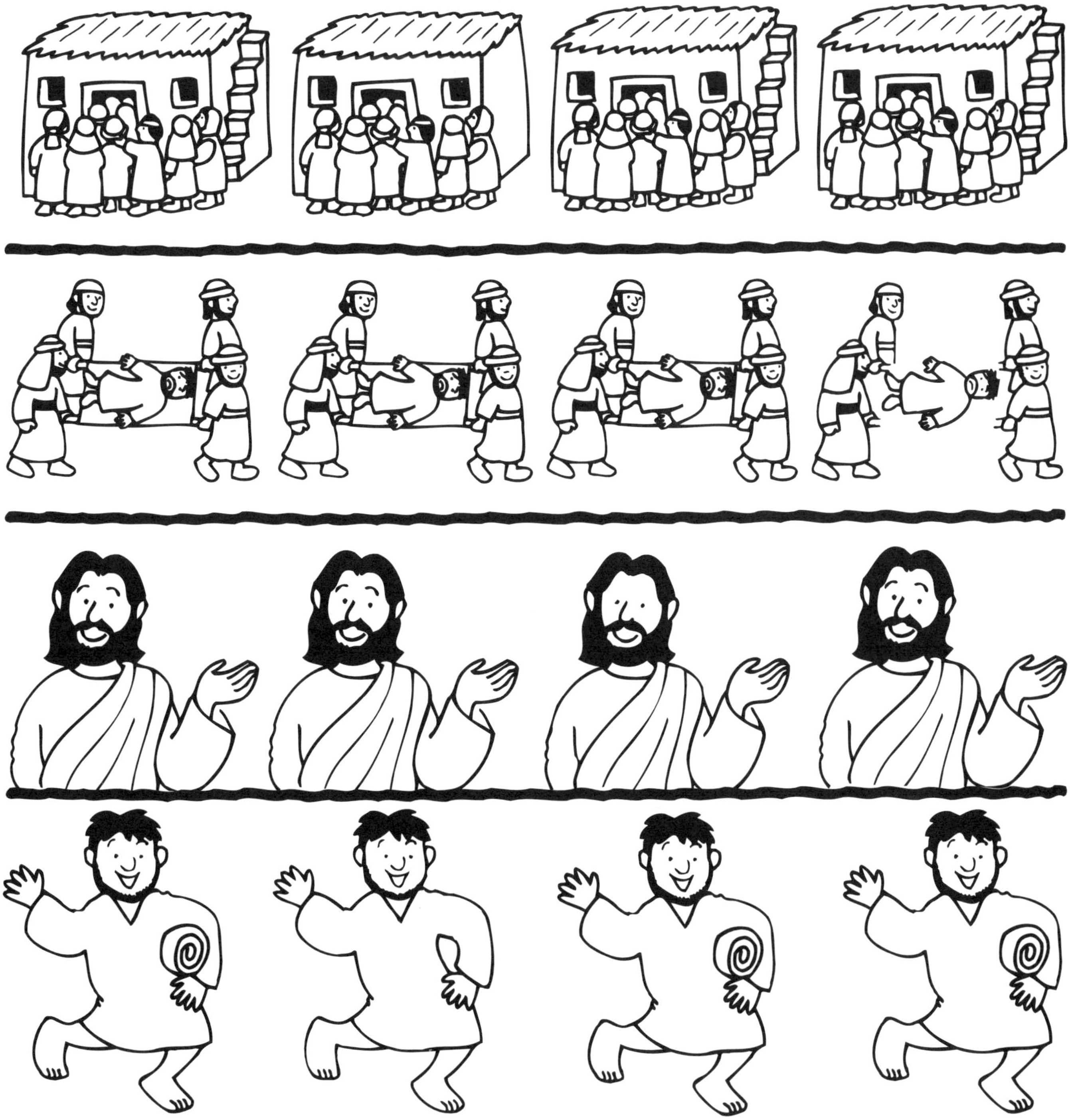

Four kind men brought their friend to see Jesus.
We can be kind to others, too.
Our Bible says, "Always try to be kind to each other." 1 Thessalonians 5:15

Below each letter write the letter that comes after it in the alphabet.

j	h	m	c

You can spell **kind**!
Find and draw a ○ around that word in the Bible verse.

Draw an ✖ on the silly things in this picture.
(There are at least 9!)
Draw a ◯ around the children who are being kind.

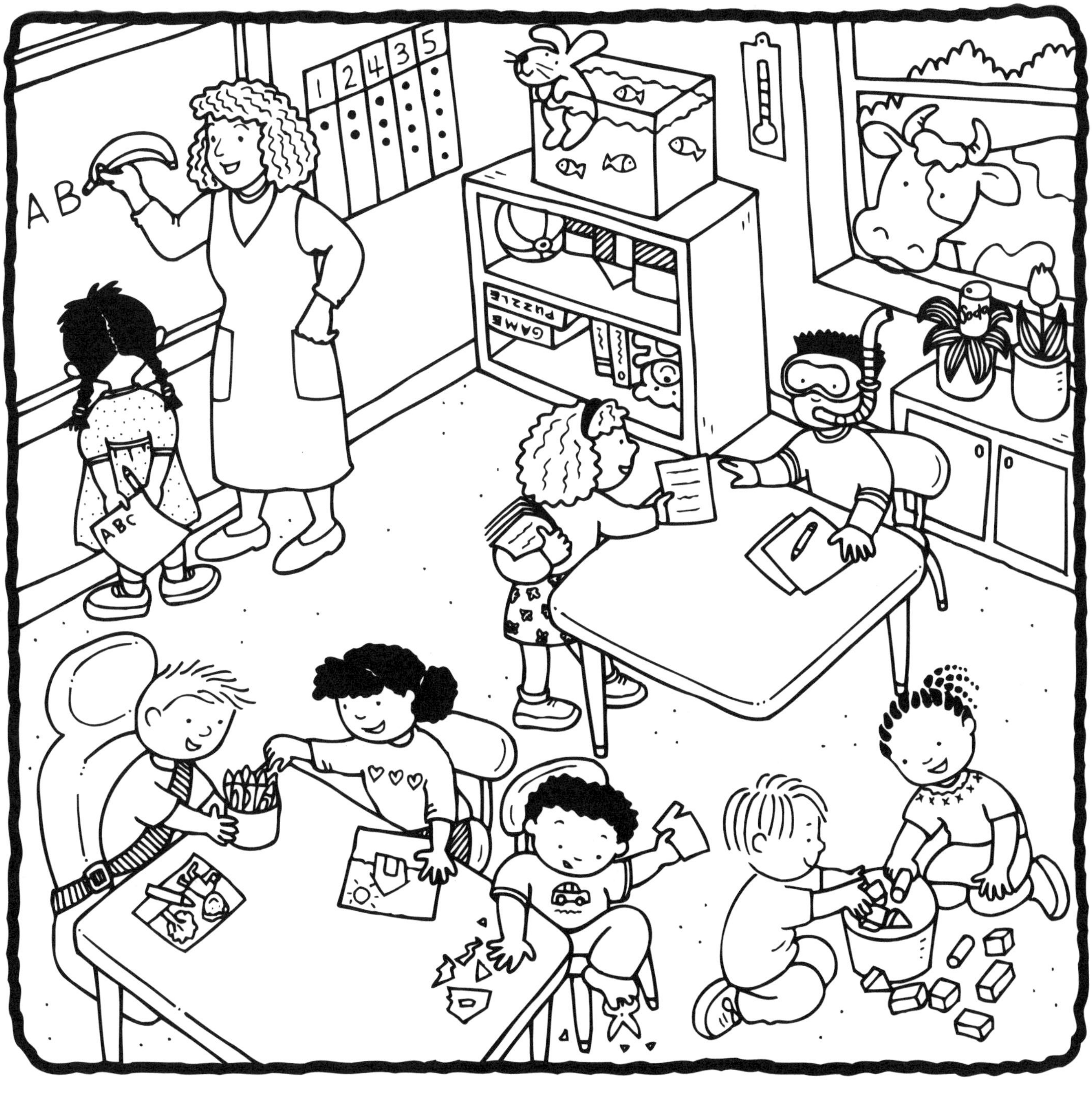

Jesus teaches us to be kind to one another.
Our Bible says, "Always try to be kind to each other." 1 Thessalonians 5:15

Look at the picture. Try to remember everything you see.
Then turn the page over. Name as many silly things as you can remember.
Look at the picture again, and then turn the page.
Name the kind actions the children were doing.

When Jesus made these men well, only one man thanked Him.

Draw a ○ around the man who thanked Jesus:

1. His arms are above his head.
2. He is wearing sandals.
3. He is smiling.

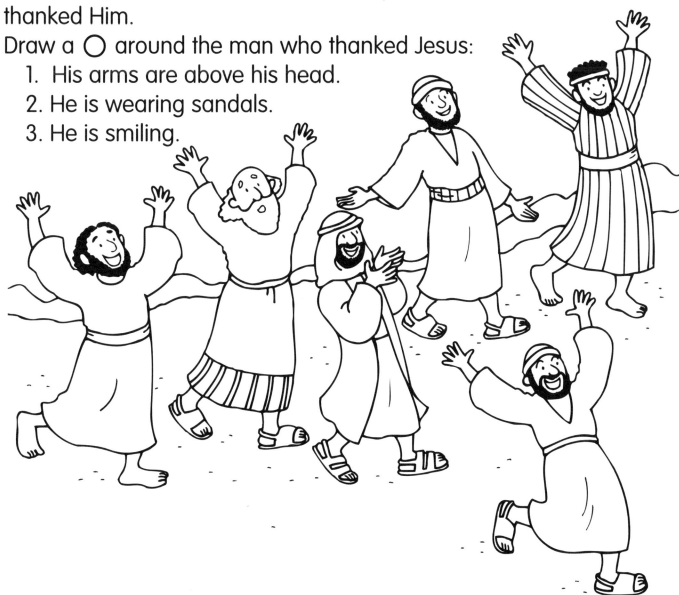

We can thank Jesus, too.

Our Bible says, "I will give thanks to the Lord." Psalm 7:17

Jesus healed 10 men. How many men are in this picture? ______

How many more men do you need to add to show all the men Jesus healed? ______

Draw that many more men.

Use a different color to trace each line.
Then you will see what God has made so that we can have food.

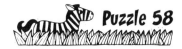

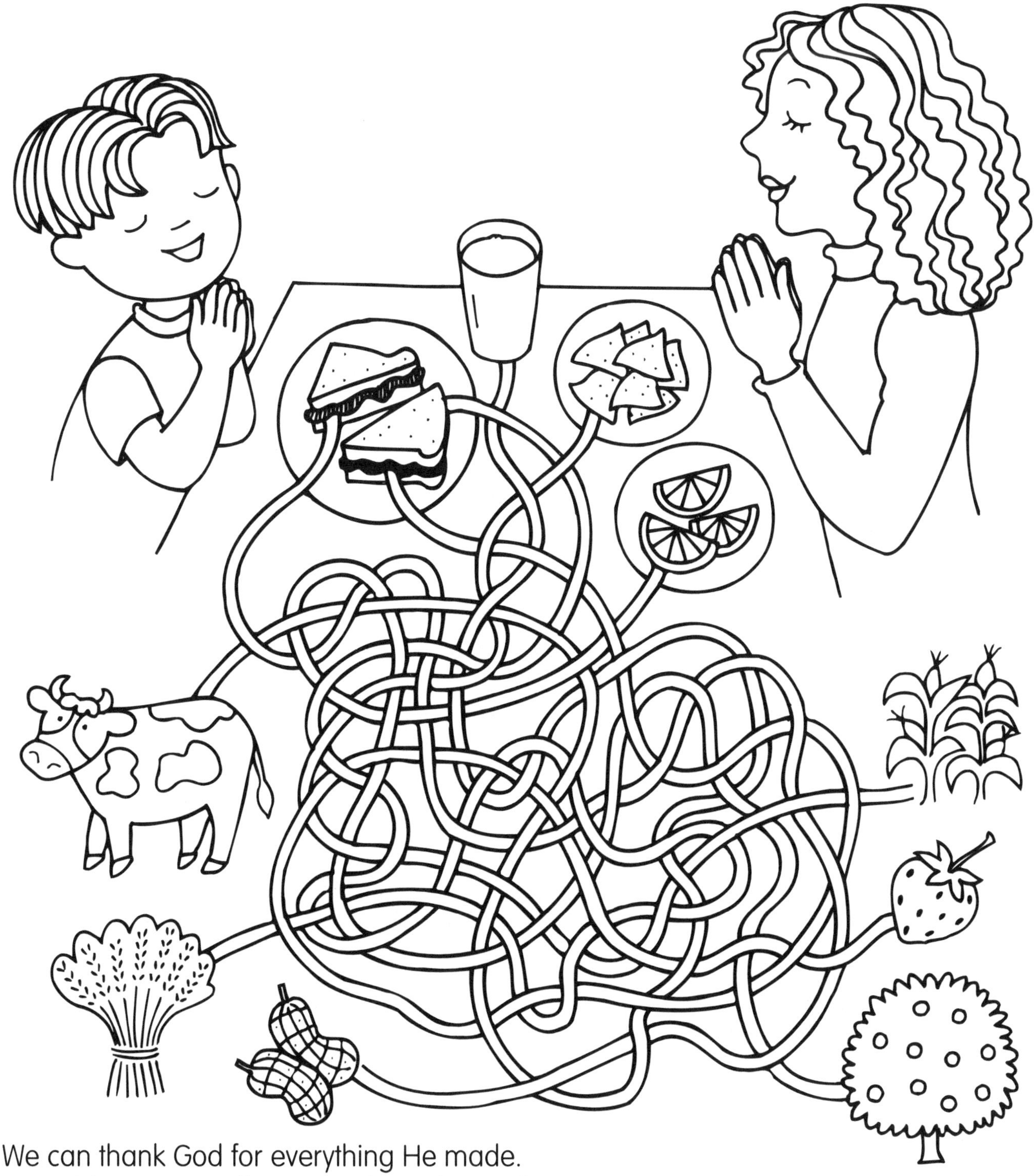

We can thank God for everything He made.
Our Bible says, "I will give thanks to the Lord." Psalm 7:17

Draw a picture of some food your family likes to eat together.
Thank God for your family.

Look at the picture to see how much a rich man in Bible times may have had.

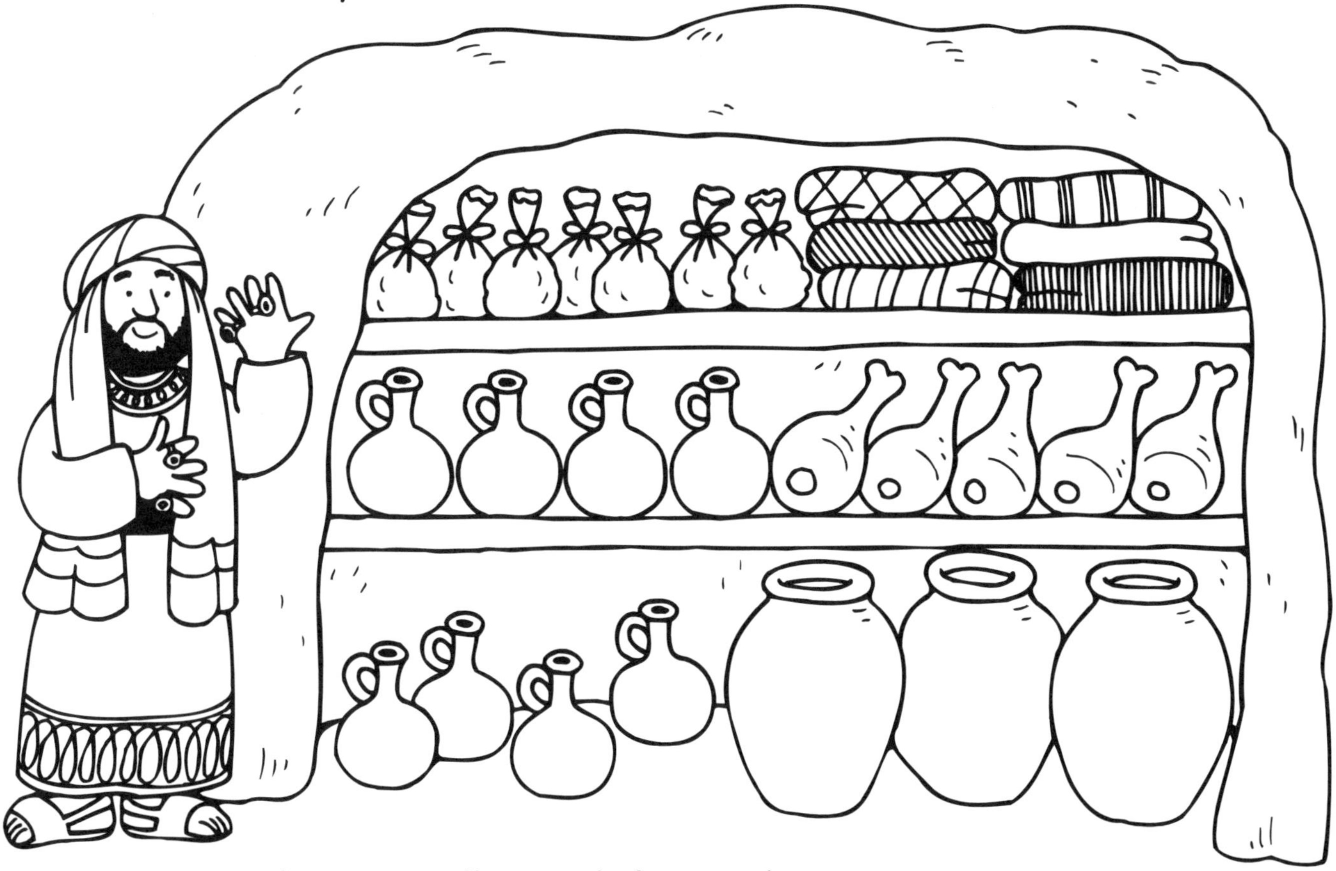

Make one tally mark for each item you count.
Write the number on the line below your tally marks.

Jesus told a rich man to share with poor people.
Jesus wants us to share, too.
Our Bible says, "Do good and be ready to share." (See 1 Timothy 6:18.)

Think of something you can share with others.
Draw a group of 7 of that item.

Draw a ◯ around the person in each room who is sharing.
In the empty room, draw a picture of someone sharing.

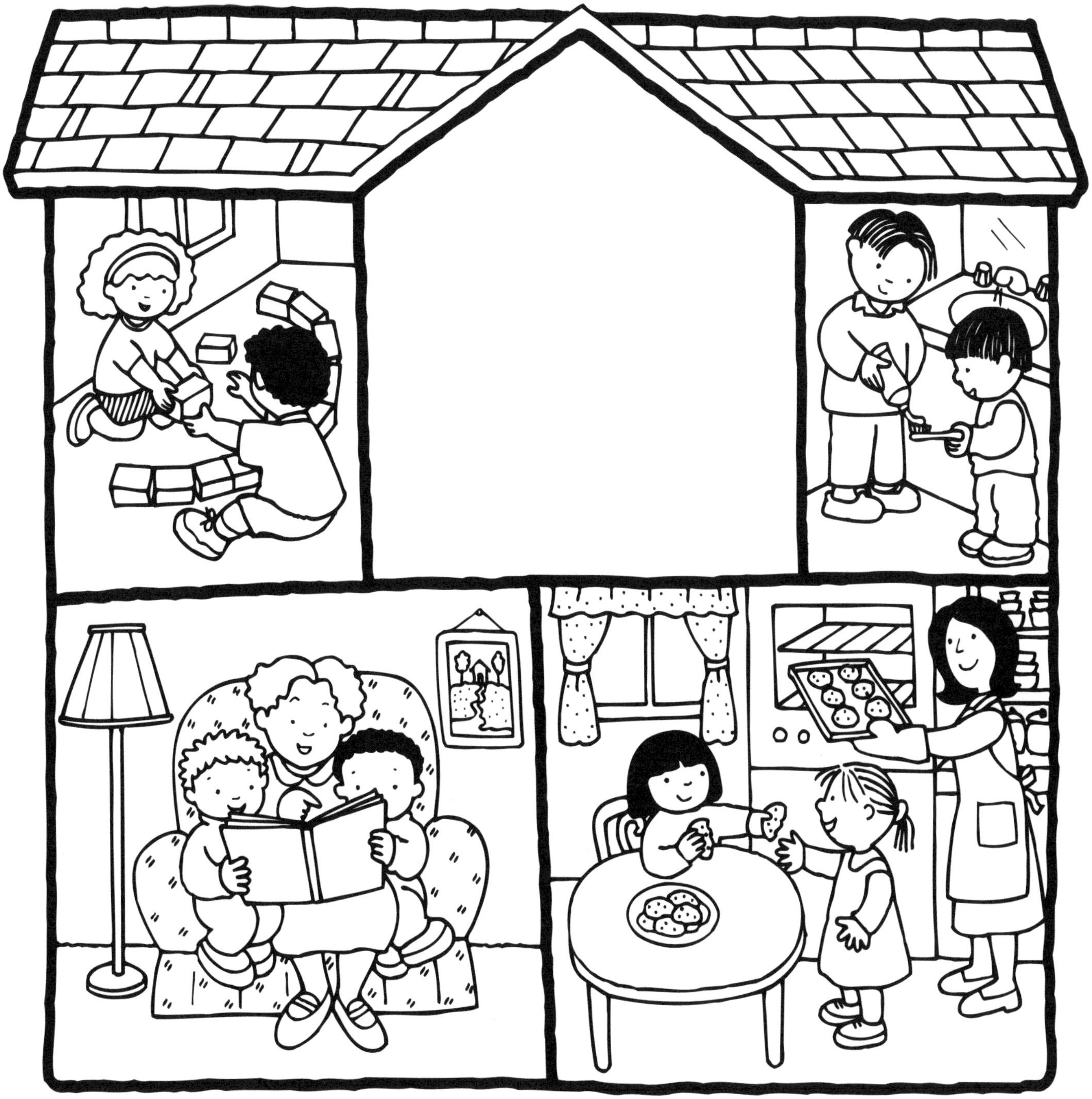

Jesus teaches us to do good to others.
Our Bible says, "Do good and be ready to share." (See 1 Timothy 6:18.)

To share, you need at least 2 people. 2 is an **even** number.
Any number that can be made into groups of 2 with none left over is **even**.
Draw a line to connect every 2 people to see if there is an **even** number of people on this page.

Trace the path to the city.
Follow this pattern:

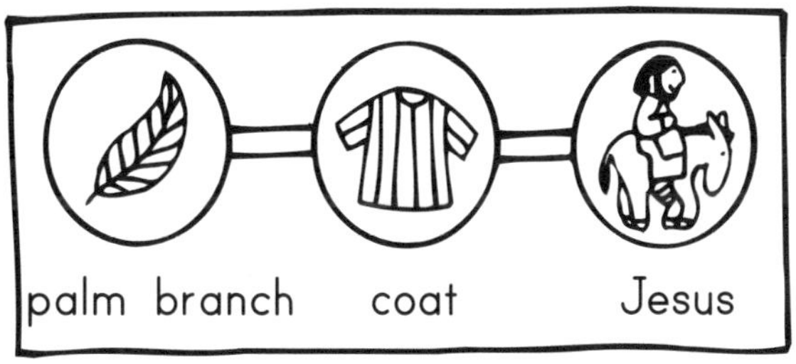

palm branch coat Jesus

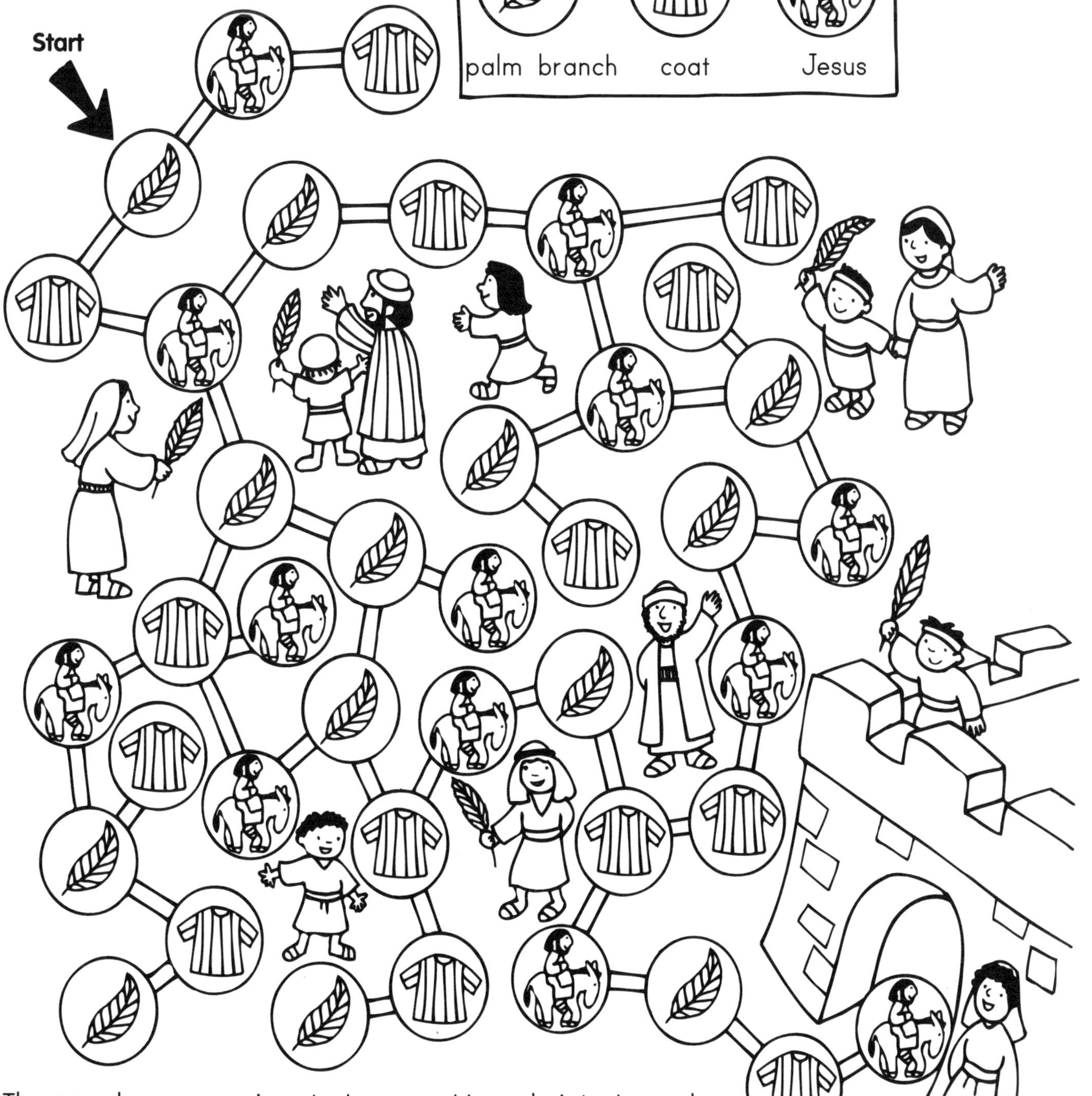

Start

The people sang praises to Jesus as He rode into Jerusalem.
We can praise Jesus, too.
Our Bible says, "How good it is to sing praises to our God." Psalm 147:1

Draw 3 pictures. Use them in a pattern to make a path.
Give it to a friend to trace.

Copy the letters from the picture onto the lines under the matching music notes and instruments.

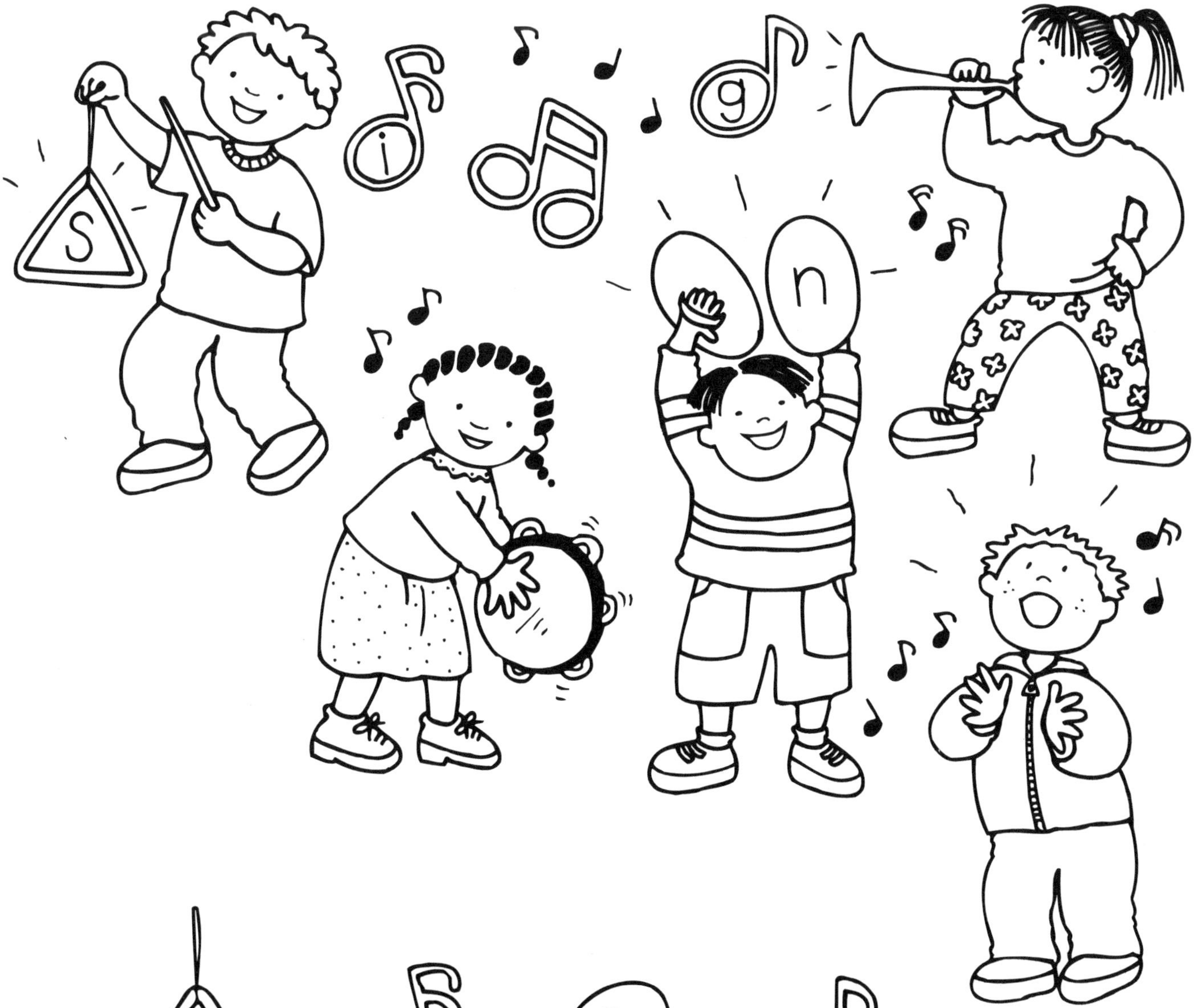

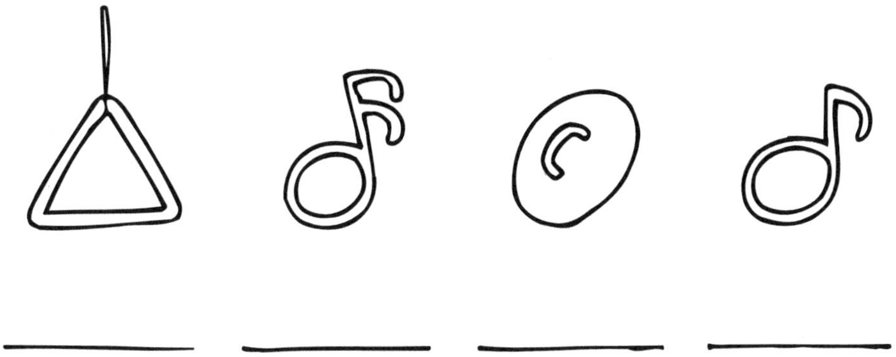

______ ______ ______ ______

We can sing praises to thank God for Jesus.
Our Bible says, "How good it is to sing praises to our God." Psalm 147:1

Draw a picture of the instrument you want to use to praise God.

Color the picture by using the correct colored crayon for each numbered space.

1-GREEN | 2-BROWN | 3-GRAY | 4-YELLOW

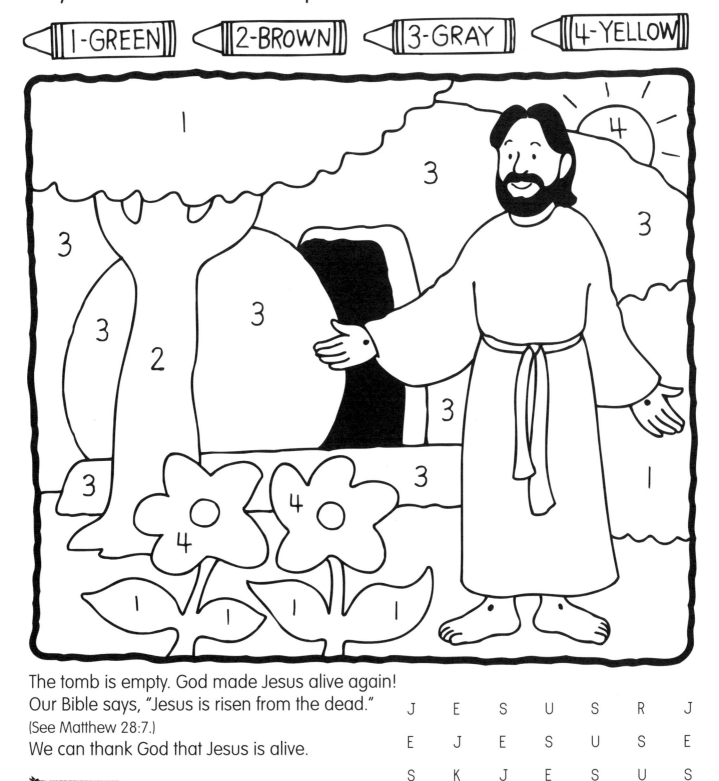

The tomb is empty. God made Jesus alive again! Our Bible says, "Jesus is risen from the dead." (See Matthew 28:7.) We can thank God that Jesus is alive.

Draw a ◯ around JESUS' name every place you find it in this puzzle.

J	E	S	U	S	R	J
E	J	E	S	U	S	E
S	K	J	E	S	U	S
U	B	V	U	E	P	U
S	U	S	E	J	C	S

Write the beginning sound of each picture to find something you can say.

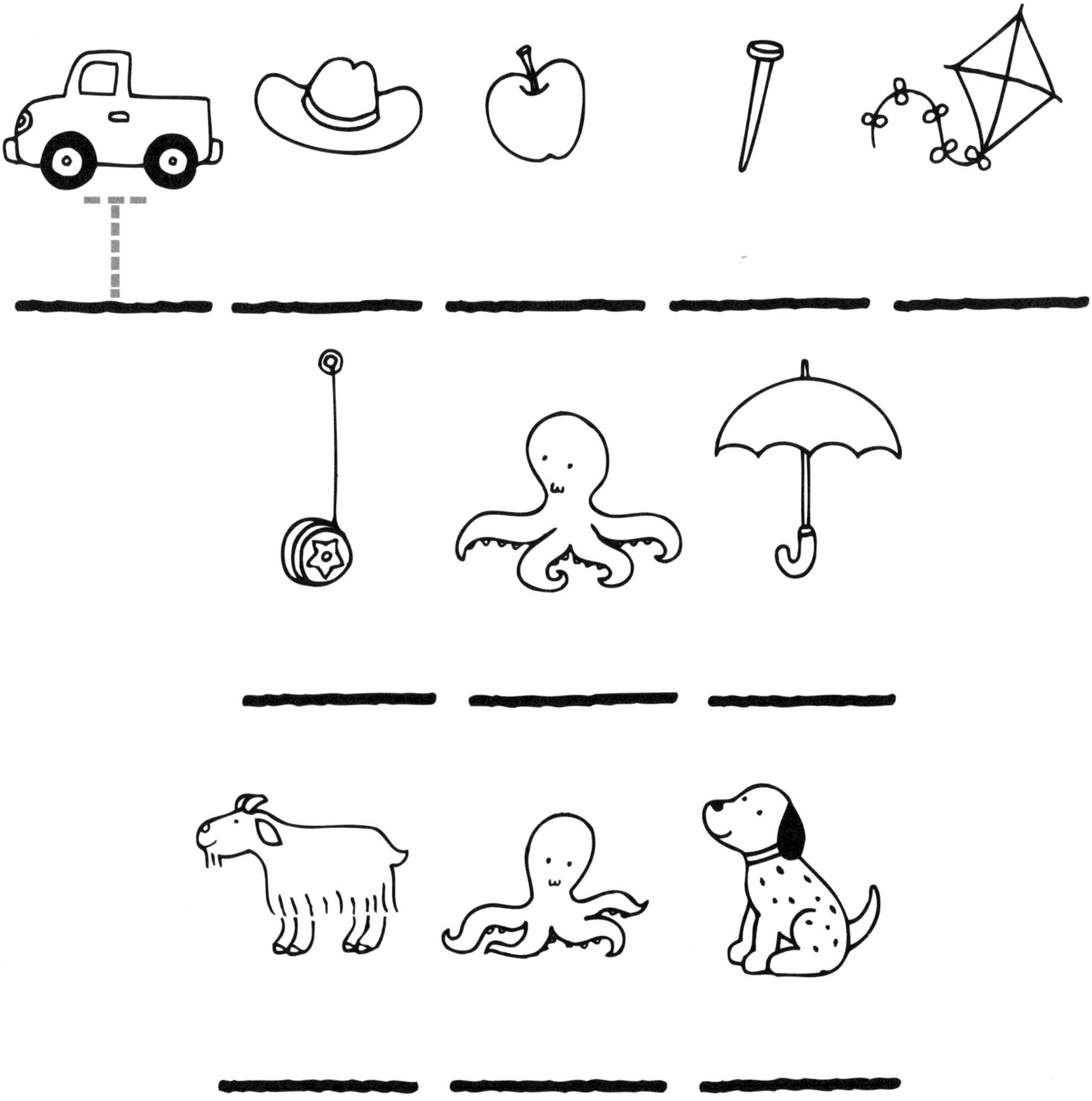

T ___ ___ ___ ___

___ ___ ___

___ ___ ___

We can thank God for many things.
We can thank God that Jesus is alive!
Our Bible says, "Jesus is risen from the dead." (See Matthew 28:7.)

Draw pictures that begin with the same sound as each letter in your name.
Draw a ★ by 2 pictures that show something you want to thank God for.

Draw lines to connect the 3 things that belong in each group.

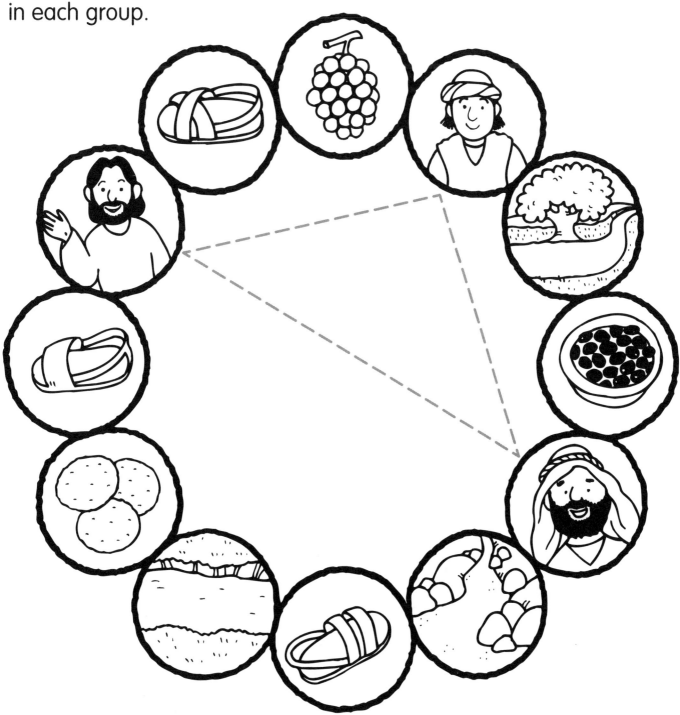

Jesus walked and talked with His friends.
They were glad Jesus was with them.
Jesus is with us, too.
Our Bible says, "Thanks be to God for Jesus." (See 2 Corinthians 9:15.)

Use the same color to color each group of 3 pictures.
Then draw 1 more picture that belongs with each group.

Fill in the blanks with the missing letters to find out the places these pictures show.

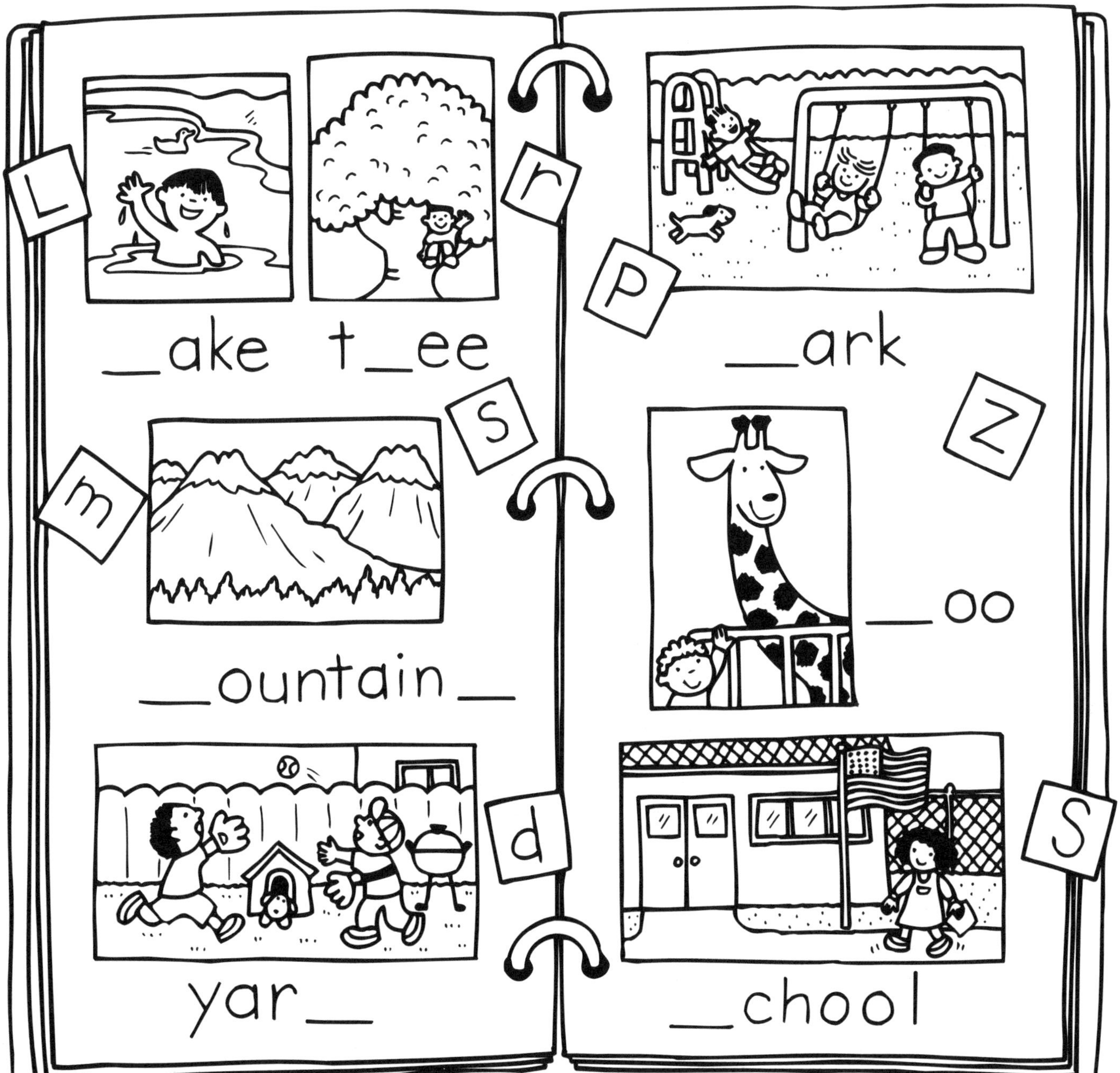

L r P s m Z d S

__ake t__ee

__ark

__ountain__

__oo

yar__

__chool

We can thank God that Jesus is with us everywhere we go.
Our Bible says, "Thanks be to God for Jesus." (See 2 Corinthians 9:15.)

Draw a picture of a place you have been.

Draw the missing lines in the picture.

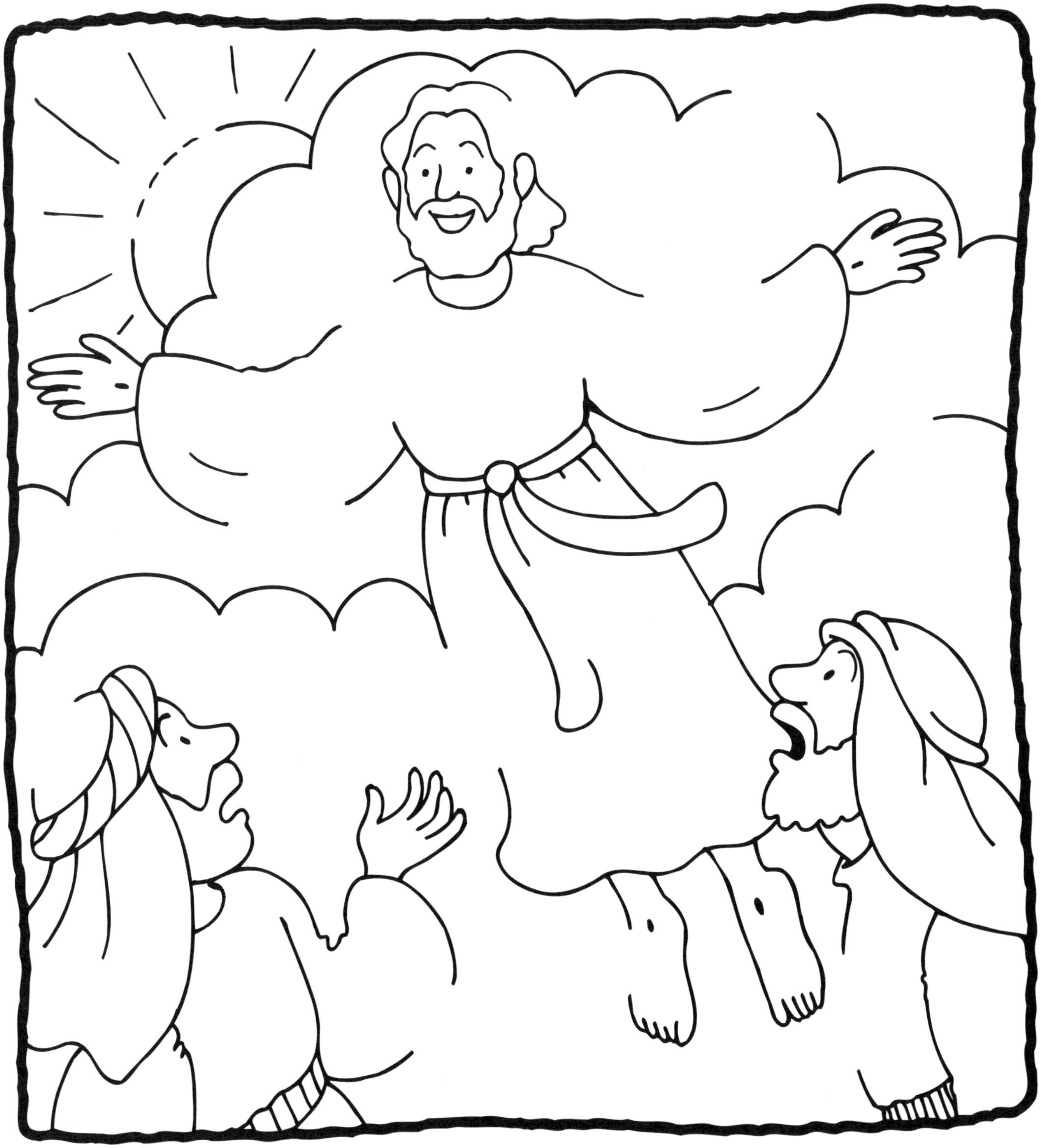

We can thank God for the good news that Jesus is alive!
Our Bible tells us, "Jesus said, 'I am alive for ever and ever!'" (See Revelation 1:18.)

How many lines did you draw in? ______
Cut this picture into that many pieces to make a puzzle.

Help the girl find her way to the picture of Jesus.

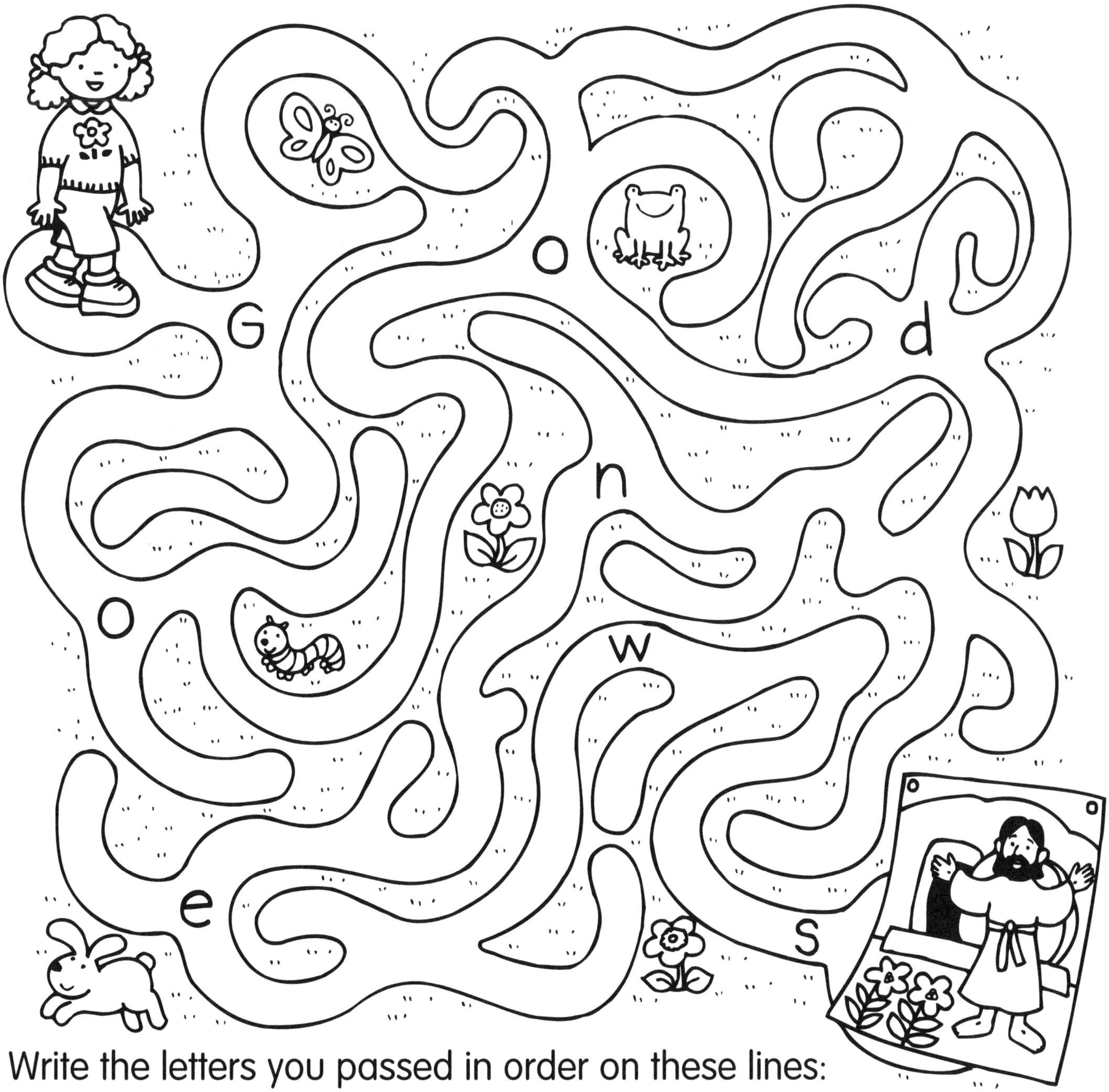

o

G

d

n

o

w

e

s

Write the letters you passed in order on these lines:

____ ____ ____ ____   ____ ____ ____ ____

Say these words out loud.
We can thank God for the good news that Jesus is alive!
Our Bible tells us, "Jesus said, 'I am alive for ever and ever!'" (See Revelation 1:18.)

Trace these letters. Then say these words out loud.

Jesus is alive.

Draw a line to connect all the boxes with pictures of people.
Don't go through any box that doesn't have a person in it.

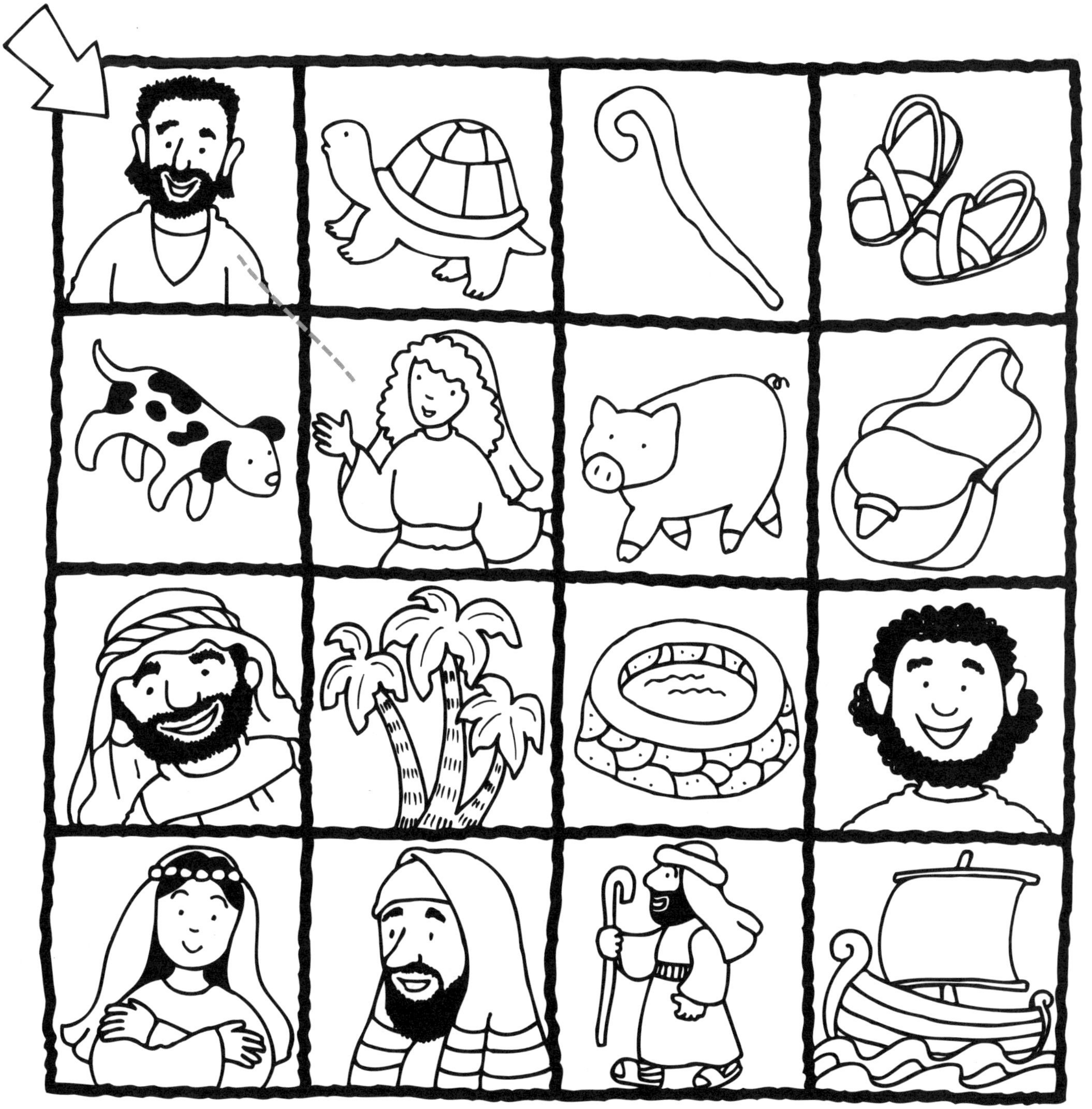

Paul told the good news about Jesus' love to many people.
We can tell other people about Jesus' love, too.
Our Bible tells us, "Jesus said, 'Go and tell the good news.'" (See Mark 16:15.)

How many people are wearing something on their head? _____ Color them RED.
How many people are not? _____ Color them BROWN.

Draw lines to match each person with a picture of the same person from a different view.

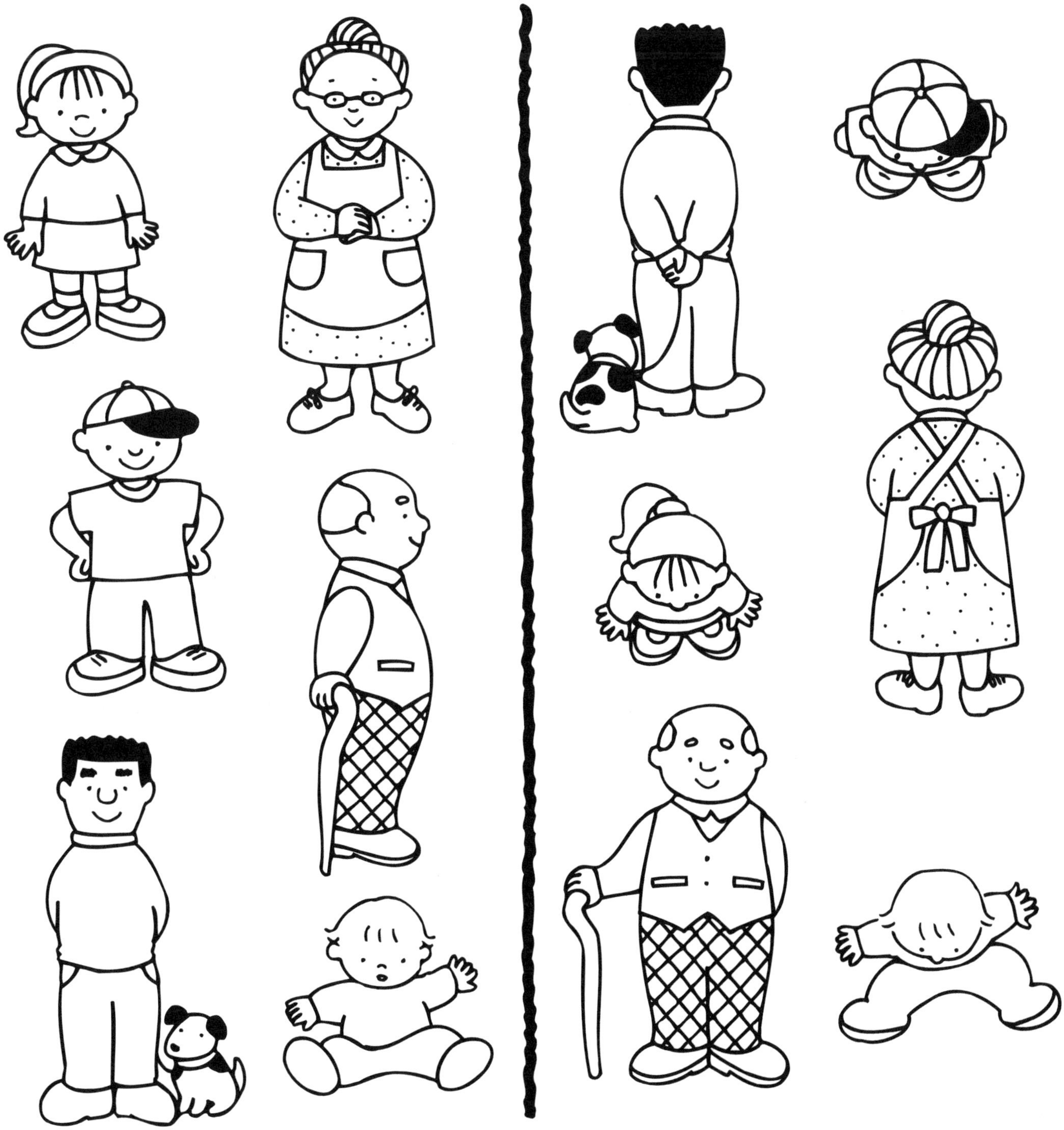

We can tell everyone the good news that Jesus loves them. Our Bible tells us, "Jesus said, 'Go and tell the good news.'" (See Mark 16:15.)

Draw a picture of someone you can tell the good news to. Then draw that person from a different view.

Look at the pictures of Paul and Silas singing in jail.
Color the 2 pictures that are exactly the same.

Paul and Silas sang songs to God and thanked Him.
We can sing songs that tell about God and all He has done, too.
Our Bible says, "Sing to God; tell of all his wonderful acts." (See Psalm 105:2.)

Make up a song about God or sing a song you know about God.

Use the pictures and words below to fill in the crossword puzzle.

Jesus

Sing

tell

We can sing songs that tell about Jesus and all the good things He has done. Our Bible says, "Sing to God; tell of all his wonderful acts." (See Psalm 105:2.)

Color and then cut out this bookmark. Use it as a reminder to thank God!

Color 1 square in the chart for each item of that kind that you see in the picture.

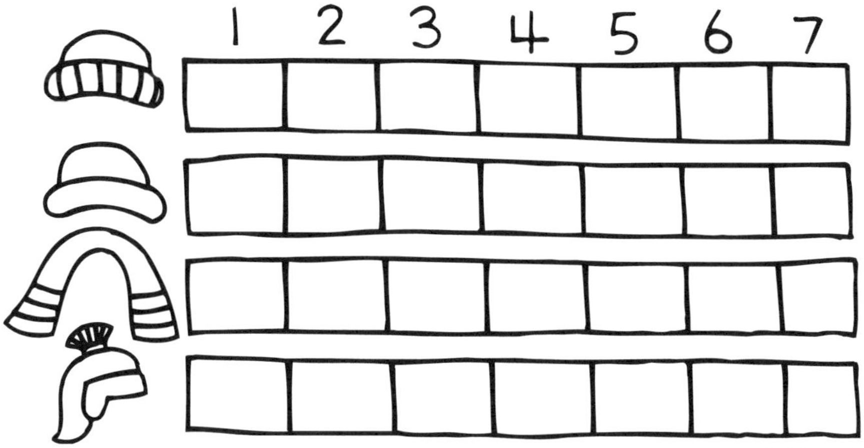

	1	2	3	4	5	6	7

Paul obeyed God's Word and told others about Jesus.
We can obey God's Word, too.
Our Bible says, "I will obey God's word." (See Psalm 119:17.)

Color all stripes that go **up and down** ||||| RED.

Color all the stripes that go **across** ≡ BLUE.

Follow the directions to see what you can do with God's Word.

1. Draw an ✖ on any numbers bigger than 5.
2. Draw an ✖ on any animals that start with an L.
3. Draw an ✖ on all the uppercase letters.

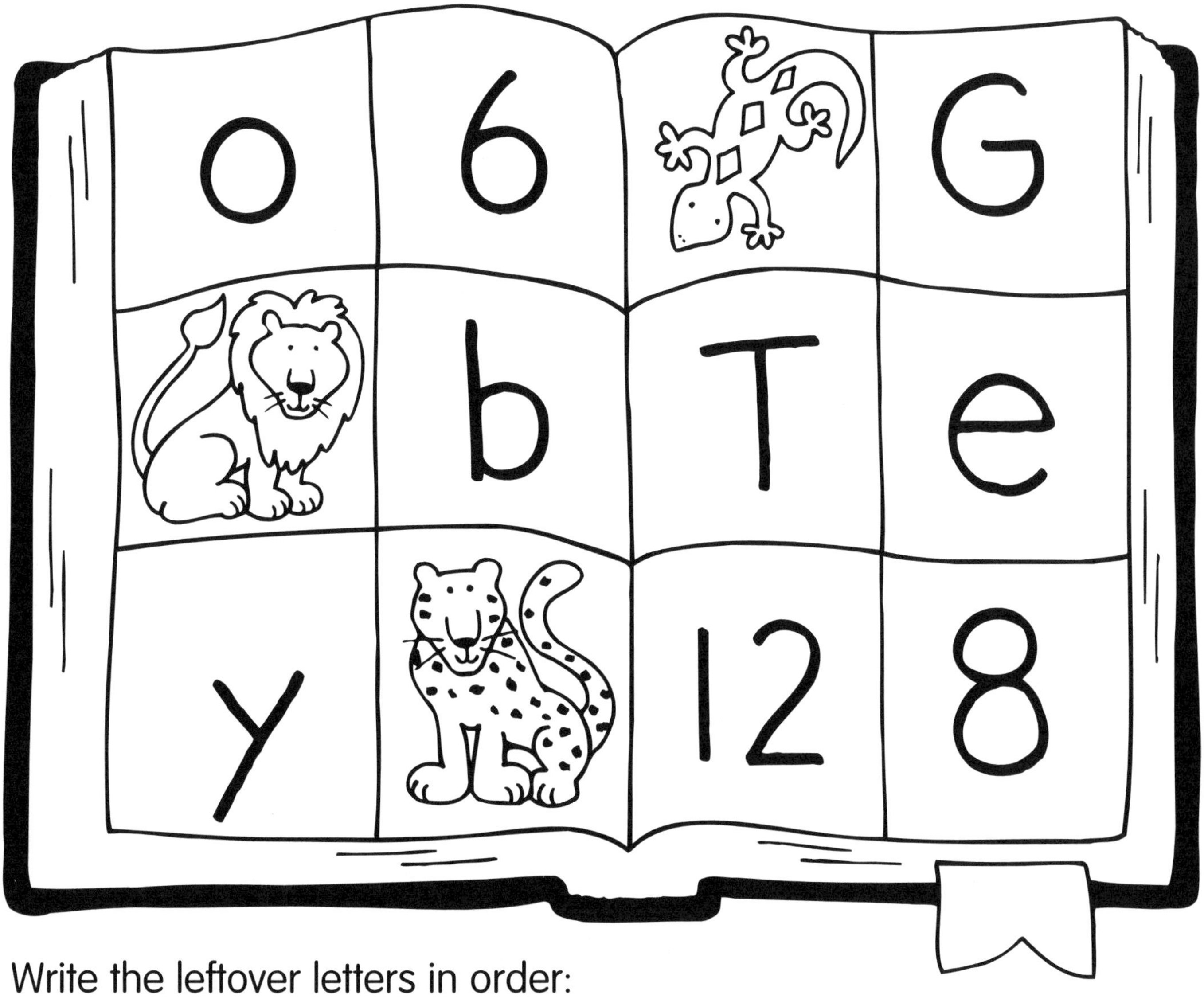

o	6		G
	b	T	e
y		12	8

Write the leftover letters in order:

______ ______ ______ ______

We can obey God's Word, the Bible.
Our Bible says, "I will obey God's word." (See Psalm 119:17.)

Cut a ○ and a △ from a sheet of paper.
Cut the ⊖ in half and put the halves on top of the ▽ to make a ♥.
We obey God's Word because we love Him!

Help Paul's nephew find his way to warn the prison guards.
Then help the guards take Paul out of the city.

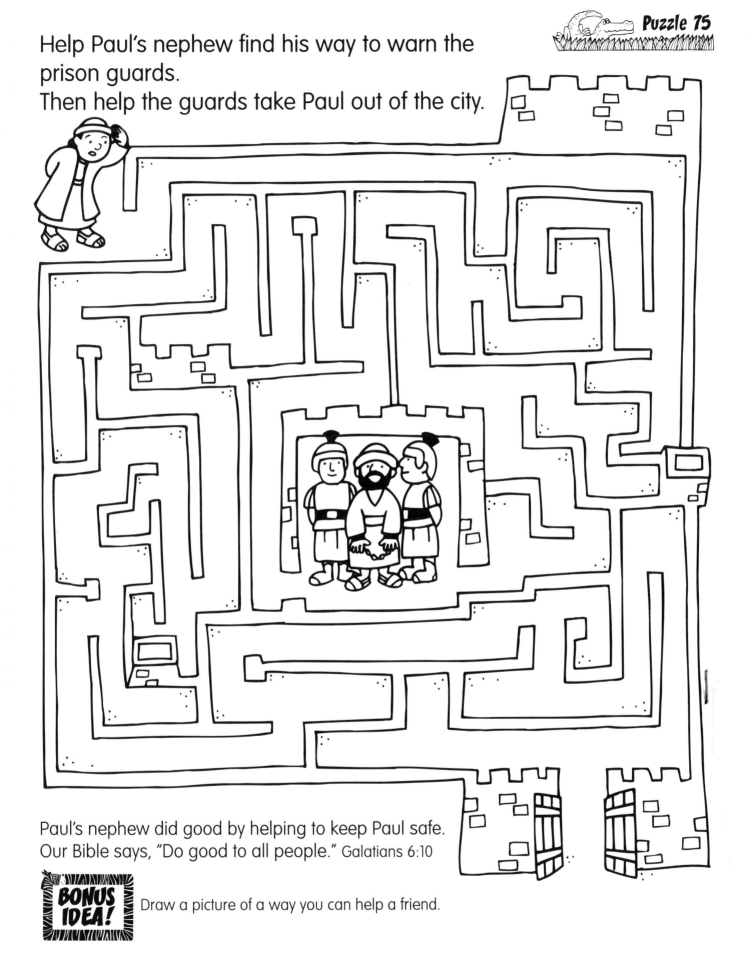

Paul's nephew did good by helping to keep Paul safe.
Our Bible says, "Do good to all people." Galatians 6:10

BONUS IDEA! Draw a picture of a way you can help a friend.

In each section, draw a ○ around the people who need help.

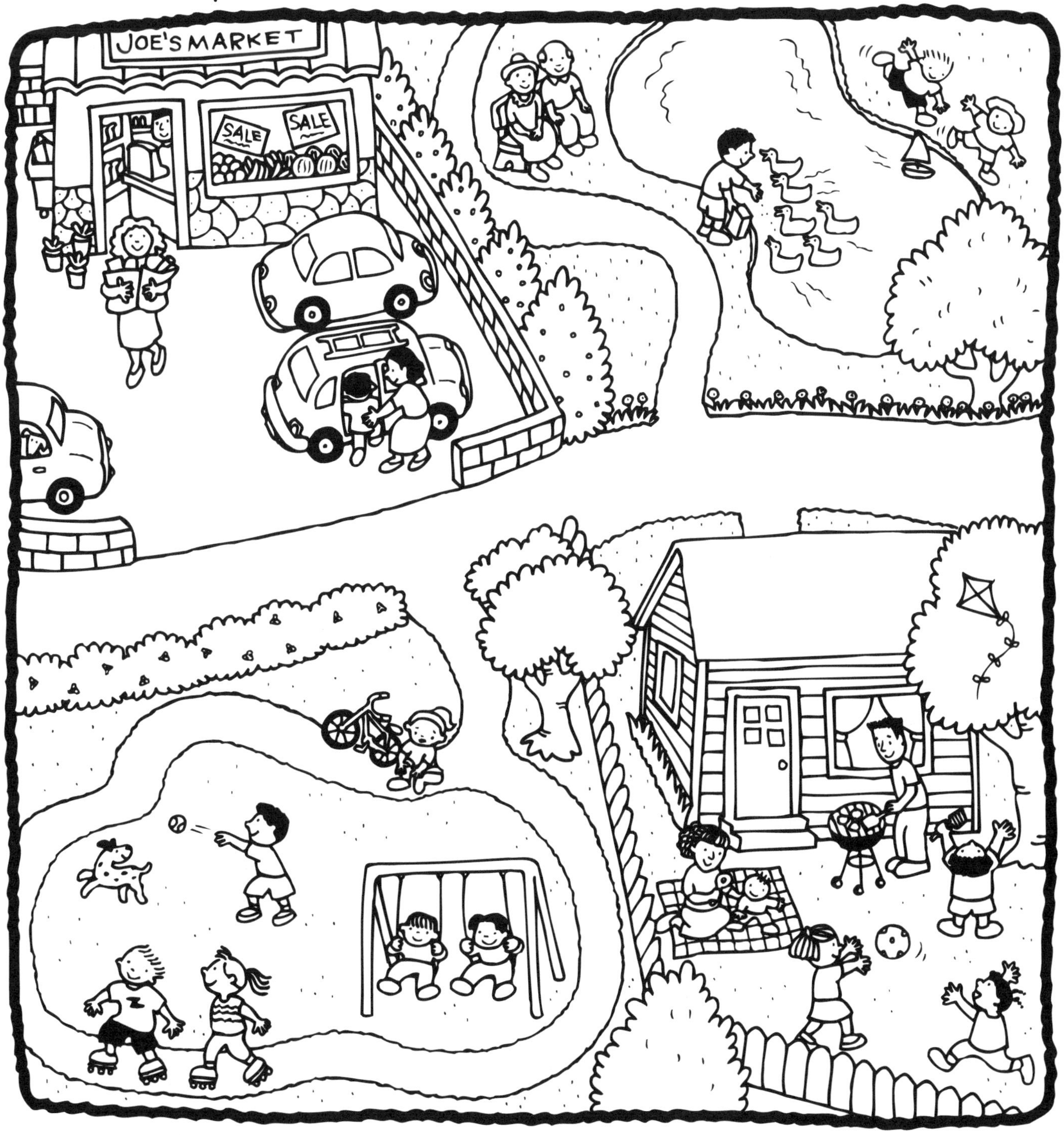

We can help others and do good to them.
Our Bible says, "Do good to all people." Galatians 6:10

Count how many people are in each section.
Write the number in the section.

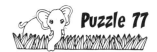

Color in everything in this picture that starts with an **S** or a **B**.
There are at least 6 things to color.

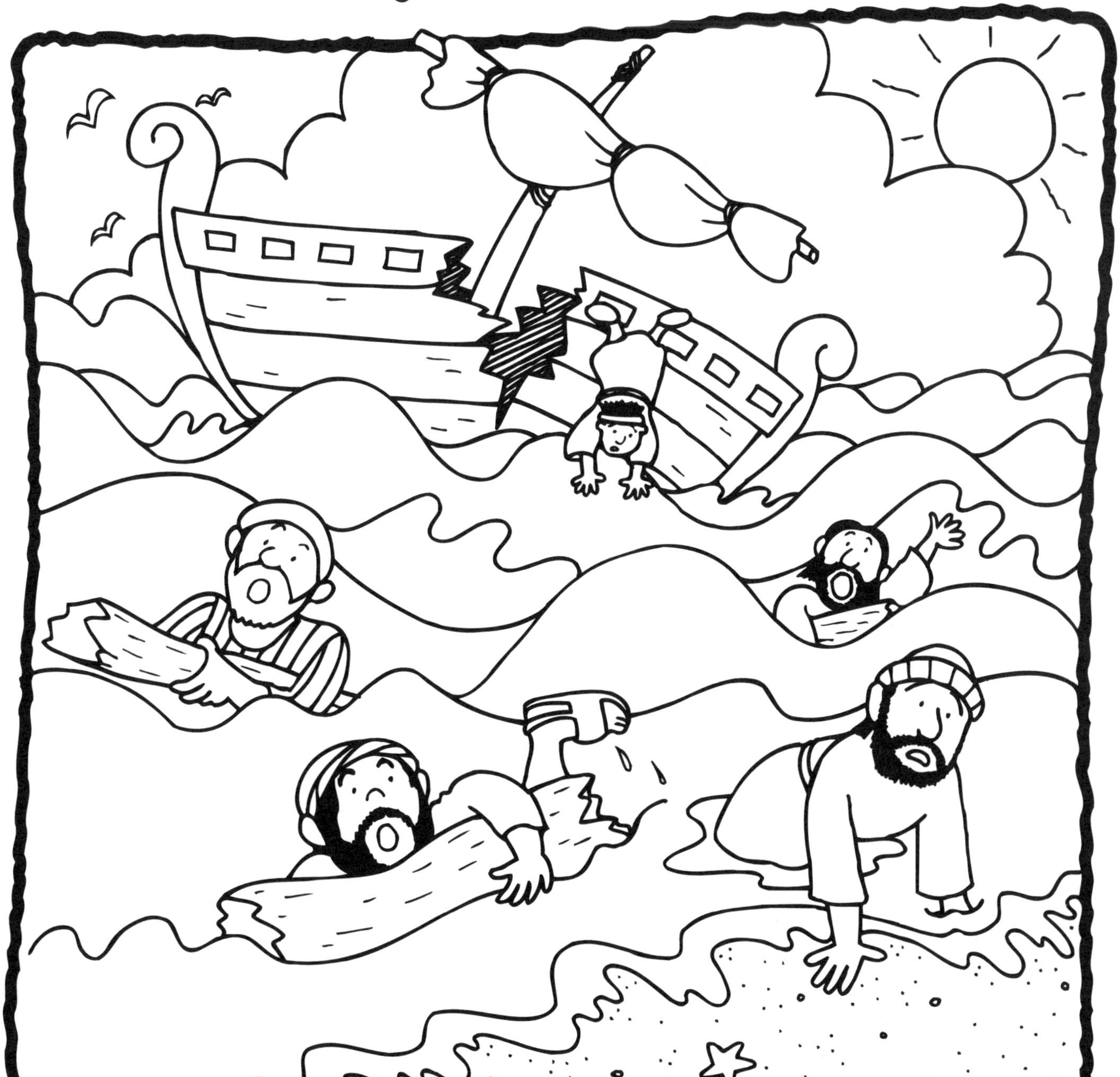

Paul showed God's love to his friends in a shipwreck.
We can show God's love to our friends, too.
Our Bible says, "A friend loves at all times." Proverbs 17:17

BONUS IDEA! Draw some things that start with a T sound.

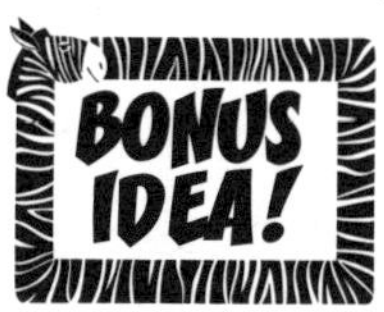

Help the boy say hello to all his friends on his way to the swing set.

We can show God's love to our friends when we play with them. Our Bible says, "A friend loves at all times." Proverbs 17:17

BONUS IDEA!

Draw a ○ around the word in each row that matches the first word. These words tell ways to show love to your friends.

share	sun	sing	share
forgive	frog	forgive	follow
help	read	hug	help

Follow the **E**'s to show Joseph's path to Egypt.

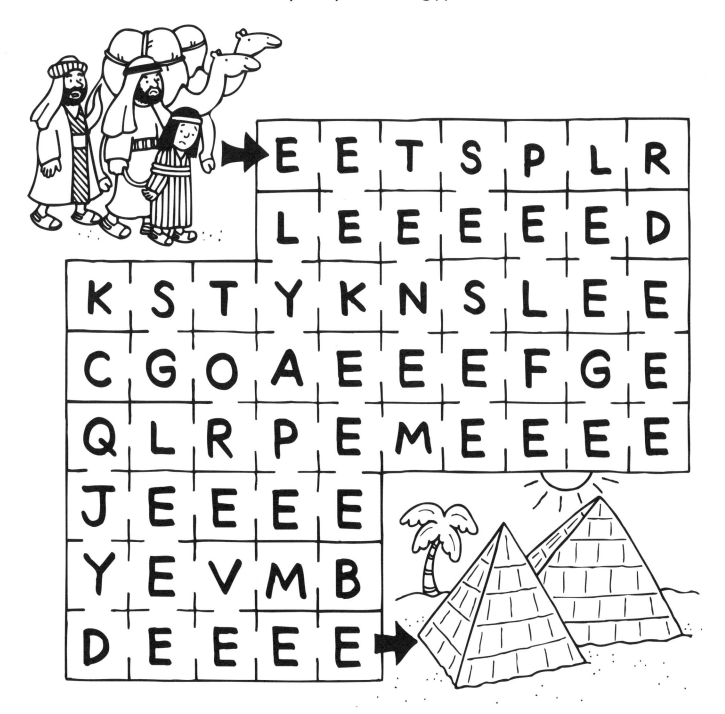

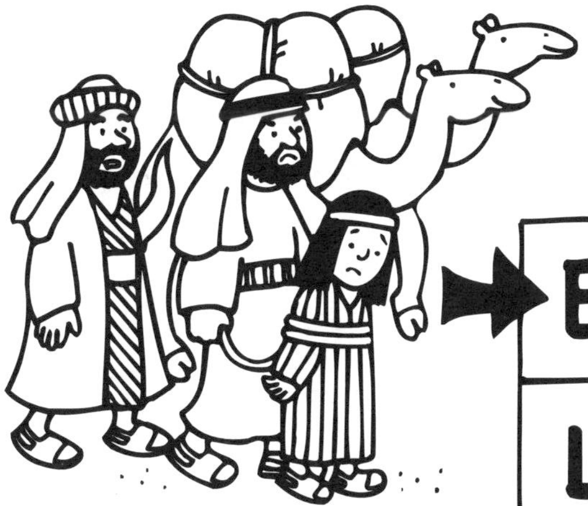

			E	E	T	S	P	L	R
			L	E	E	E	E	E	D
K	S	T	Y	K	N	S	L	E	E
C	G	O	A	E	E	E	F	G	E
Q	L	R	P	E	M	E	E	E	E
J	E	E	E	E					
Y	E	V	M	B					
D	E	E	E	E					

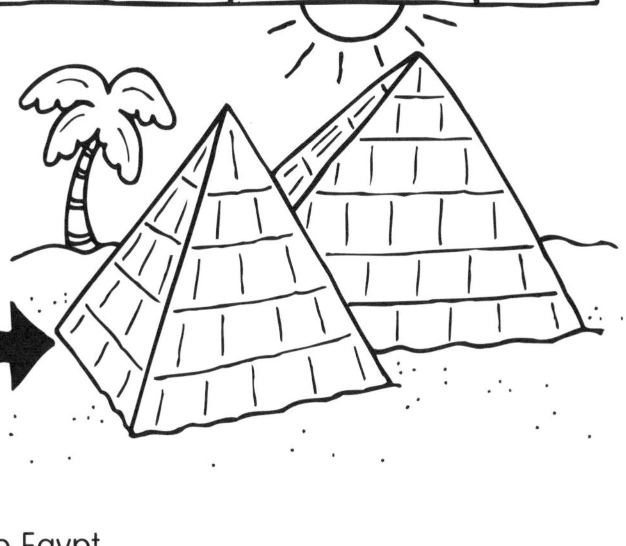

God was with Joseph when Joseph was taken to Egypt.
God is with us, too.
Our Bible says, "The Lord your God will be with you wherever you go." Joshua 1:9

Find the word GO in the maze. Copy the word.
Then add a D to the end of it. Now you've spelled GOD!

Cut out the squares and glue them where they belong in the picture.

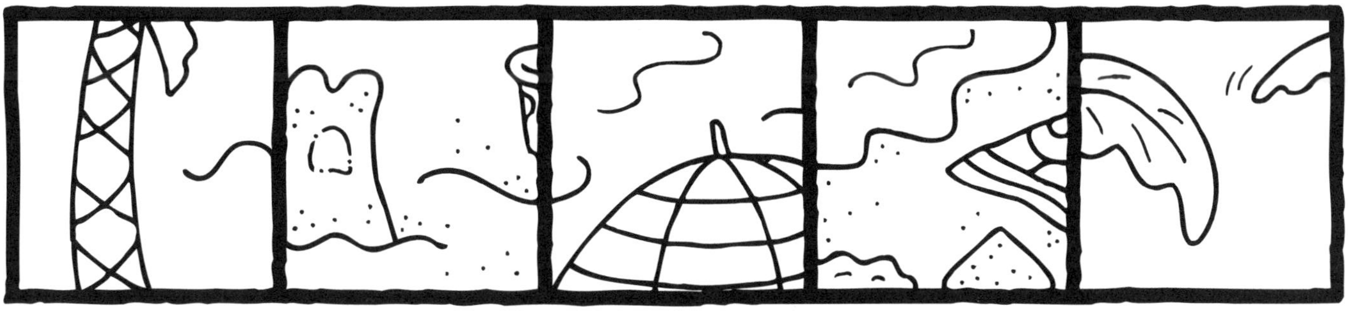

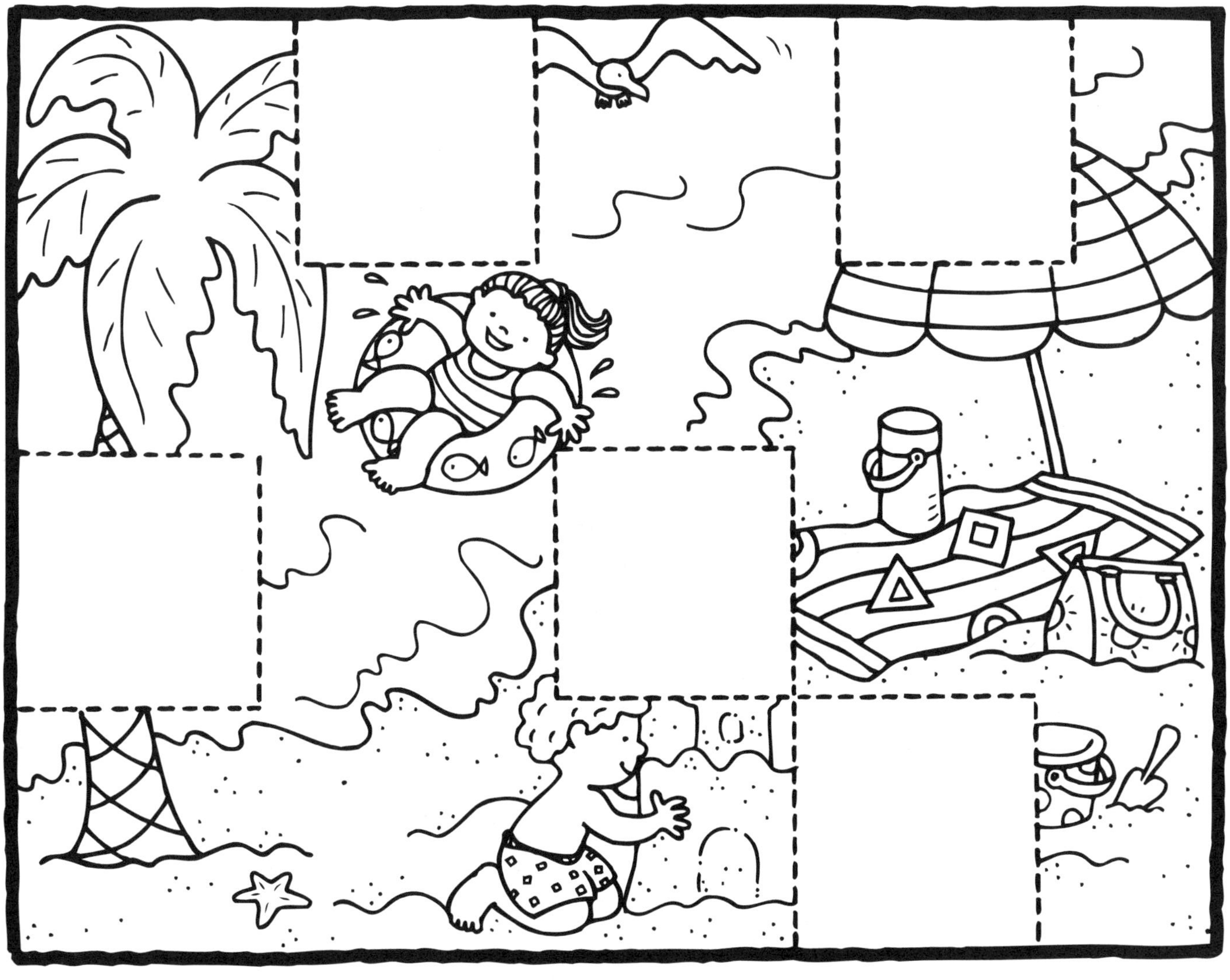

God is with us at the beach.
God is with us wherever we go.
Our Bible says, "The Lord your God will be with you wherever you go." Joshua 1:9

Draw a picture of a place you like to go.

Use BLUE to color each object in the groups of 8 or **more**.
Use ORANGE to color each object in the groups of 7 or **less**.

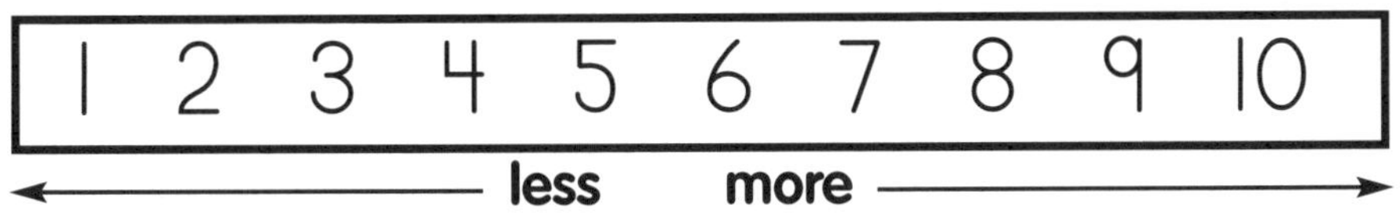

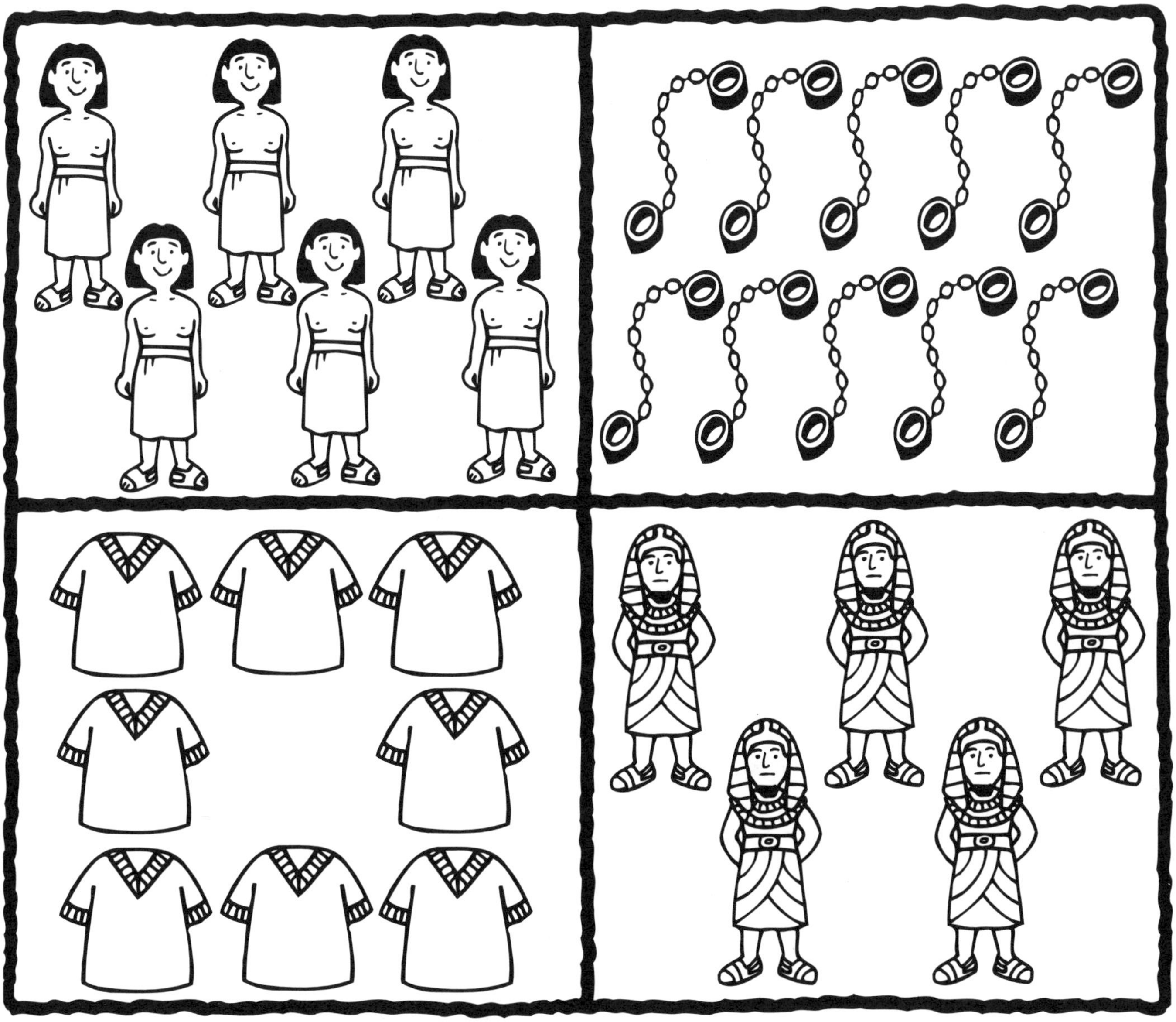

Joseph did what was right.
God will help us do what is right, too.
Our Bible says, "Don't get tired of doing what is right." (See 2 Thessalonians 3:13.)

Count how many pictures there are on the page. _______
Write a number by each picture if you need help keeping track.

Write each action word under the picture it matches.

help **share** **give** **move**

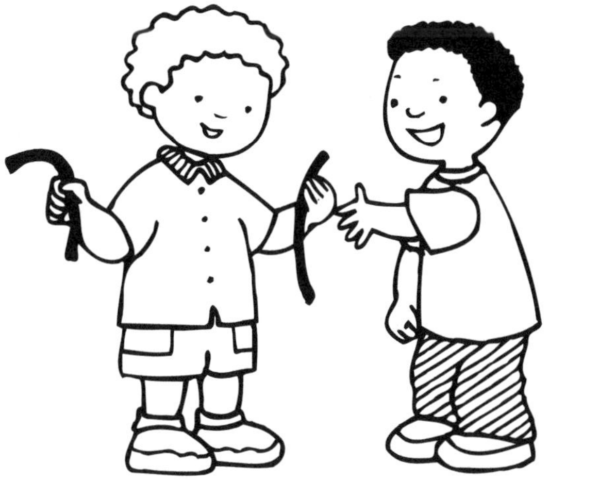

s

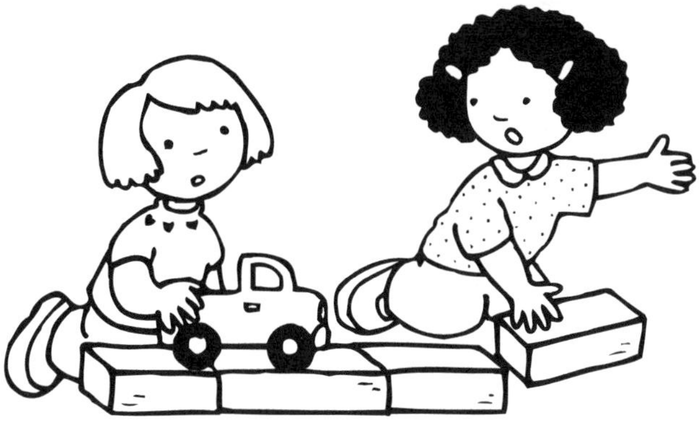

m

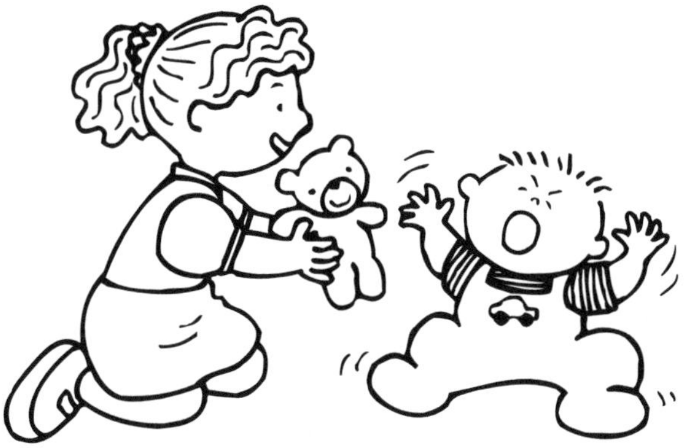

g

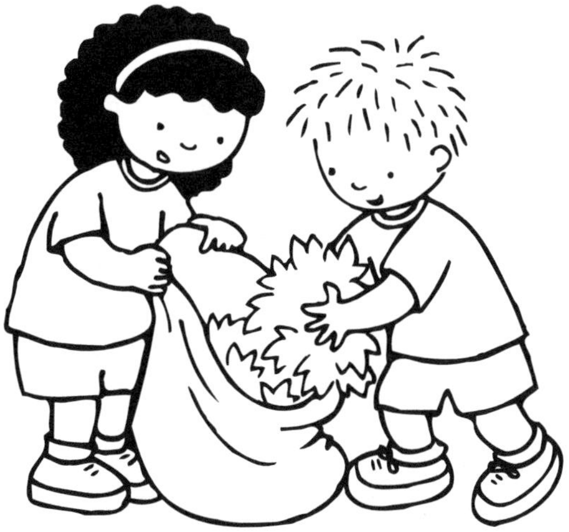

h

These pictures show ways of doing what is right.
God helps us do what is right.
Our Bible says, "Don't get tired of doing what is right." (See 2 Thessalonians 3:13.)

Look at the words you wrote. There is 1 letter that all of the words have.
Draw a O around that letter in each word.

Draw a ○ around the items hidden in the picture.

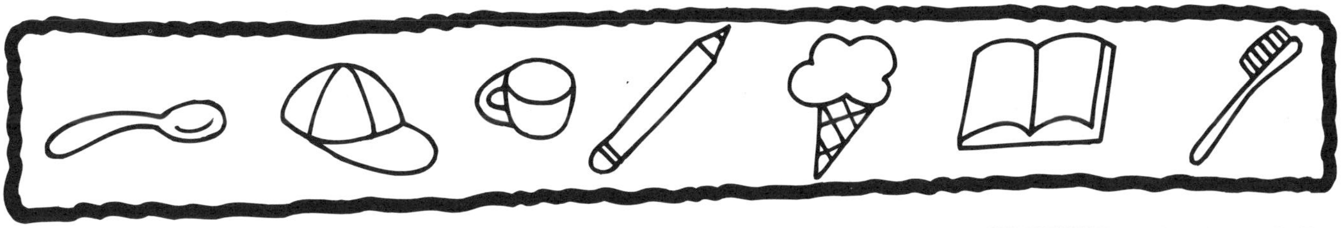

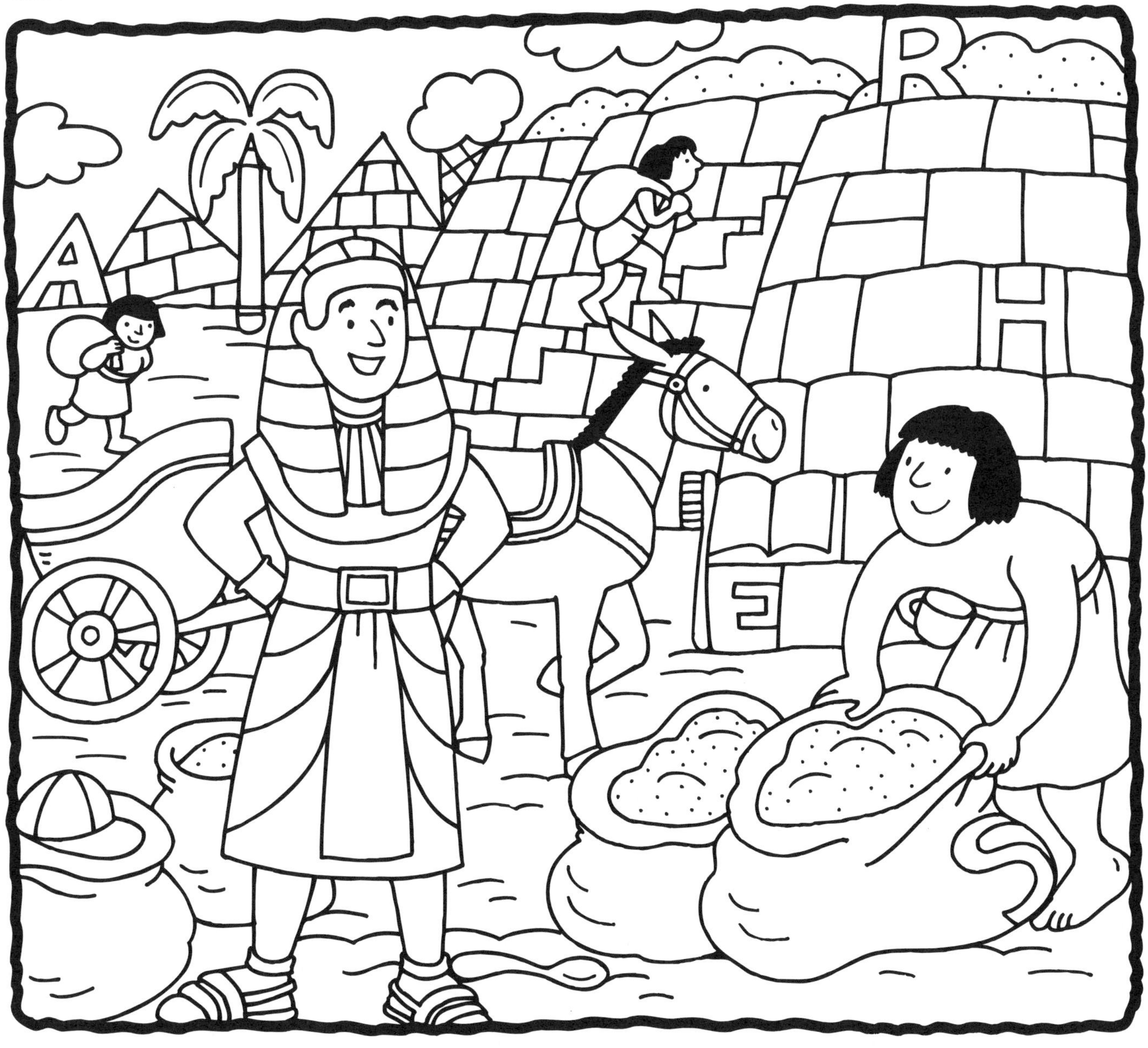

God helped Joseph save food to share.
God can help us share with others, too.
Our Bible says, "Share with God's people who are in need." Romans 12:13

Find 5 letters in the picture.
Draw a line to connect the letters to spell the word SHARE.

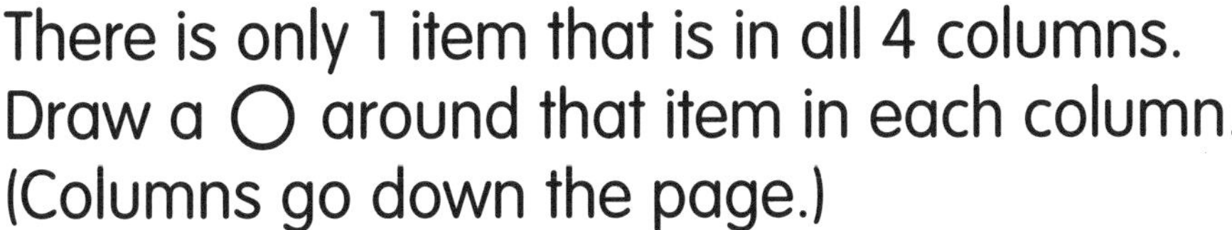

There is only 1 item that is in all 4 columns.
Draw a ○ around that item in each column.
(Columns go down the page.)

God helps us share with others.
Draw a ★ by something you have shared.
Our Bible says, "Share with God's people who are in need." Romans 12:13

What items are there 3 of? Draw a △ around those items.
What items are there 2 of? Draw a □ around those items.

Count each set and write the number.
Then draw lines connecting the sets of the same number.

1	2	3	4	5	6	7	8	9	10

4

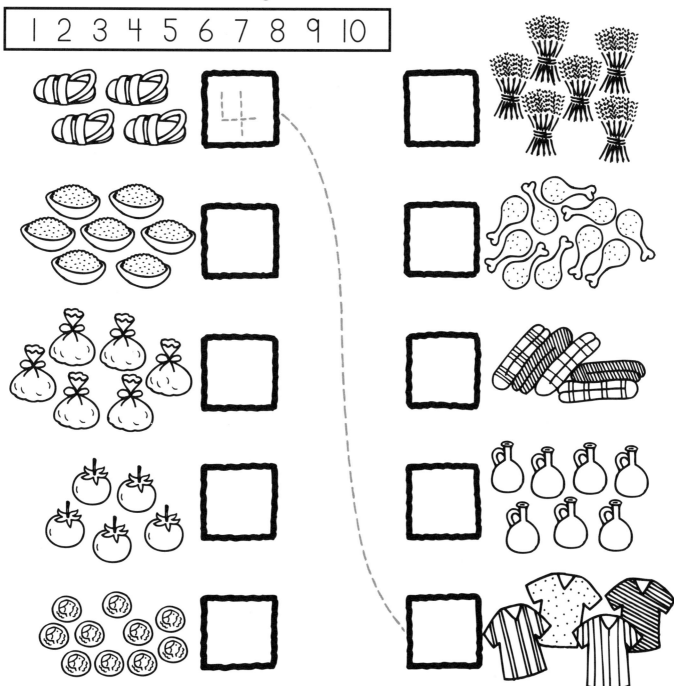

Joseph forgave his family.
He showed love for them by giving them what they needed.
God helps us show His love to others.
Our Bible says, "Love one another." John 13:34

Count the items in the sets above to complete these number sentences.

+ = ____

+ = ____

Look at the picture at the beginning of each row.
Draw a ○ around the picture of which it is a part.

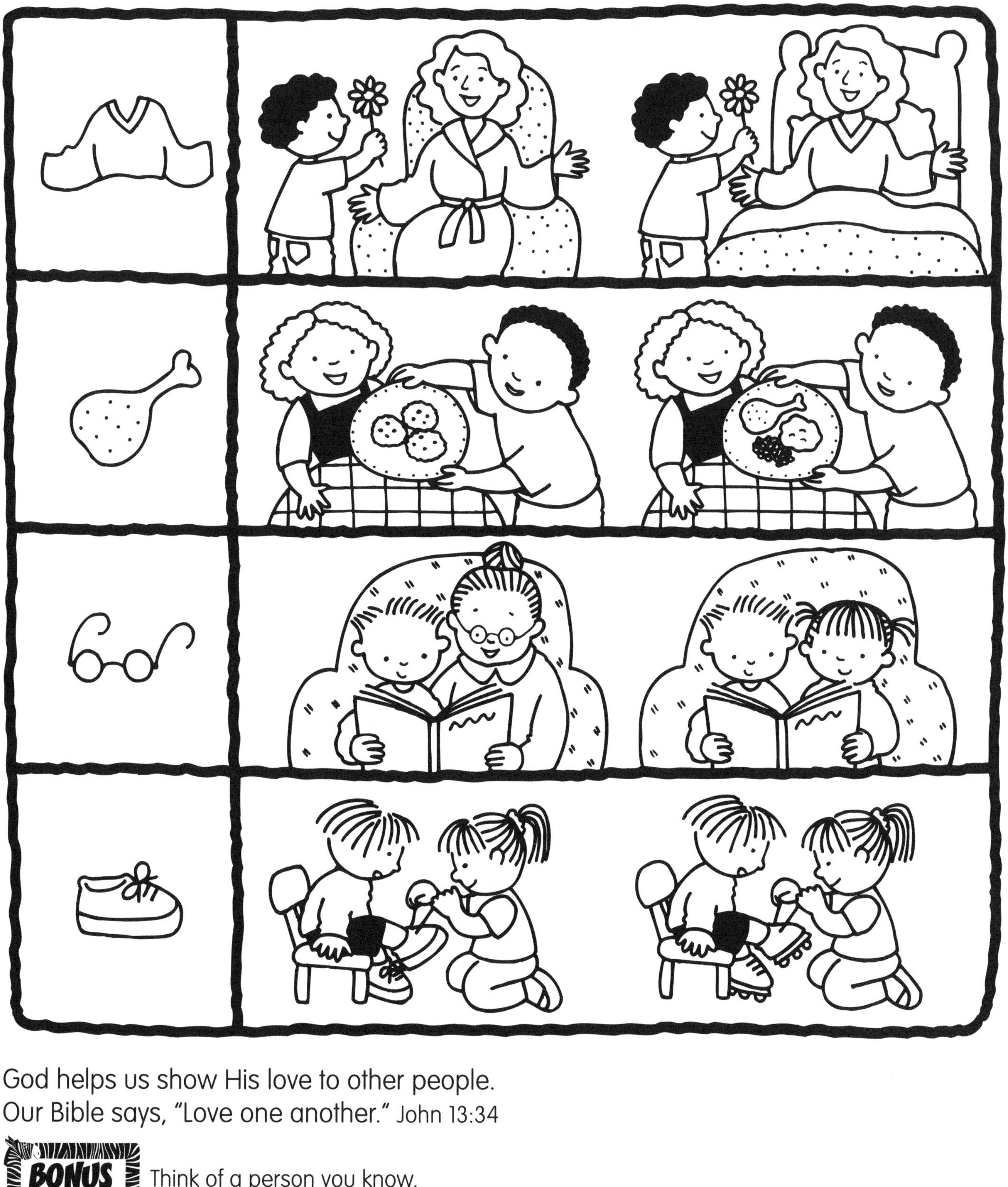

God helps us show His love to other people.
Our Bible says, "Love one another." John 13:34

Think of a person you know.
Draw a way to show God's love to that person.

In each row, draw the pictures to complete the pattern.

God cared for Elijah by giving him food to eat and water to drink.
God loves and cares for us, too.
Our Bible says, "God has been good to me." (See Genesis 33:11.)

Make a sound pattern by clapping your hands and tapping your legs.
Try this pattern: tap/tap/clap, tap/tap/clap.
What other patterns can you make?

In each row, draw a ◯ around the pictures that begin with the same sound as the letter.

Bb
Cc
Ff
Ss
Tt

God loves and cares for us by giving us people to love us and give us what we need. Our Bible says, "God has been good to me." (See Genesis 33:11.)

Draw another object that starts with the same sound as each letter.

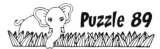

Draw a ○ around the flour and oil jugs that match the widow's.

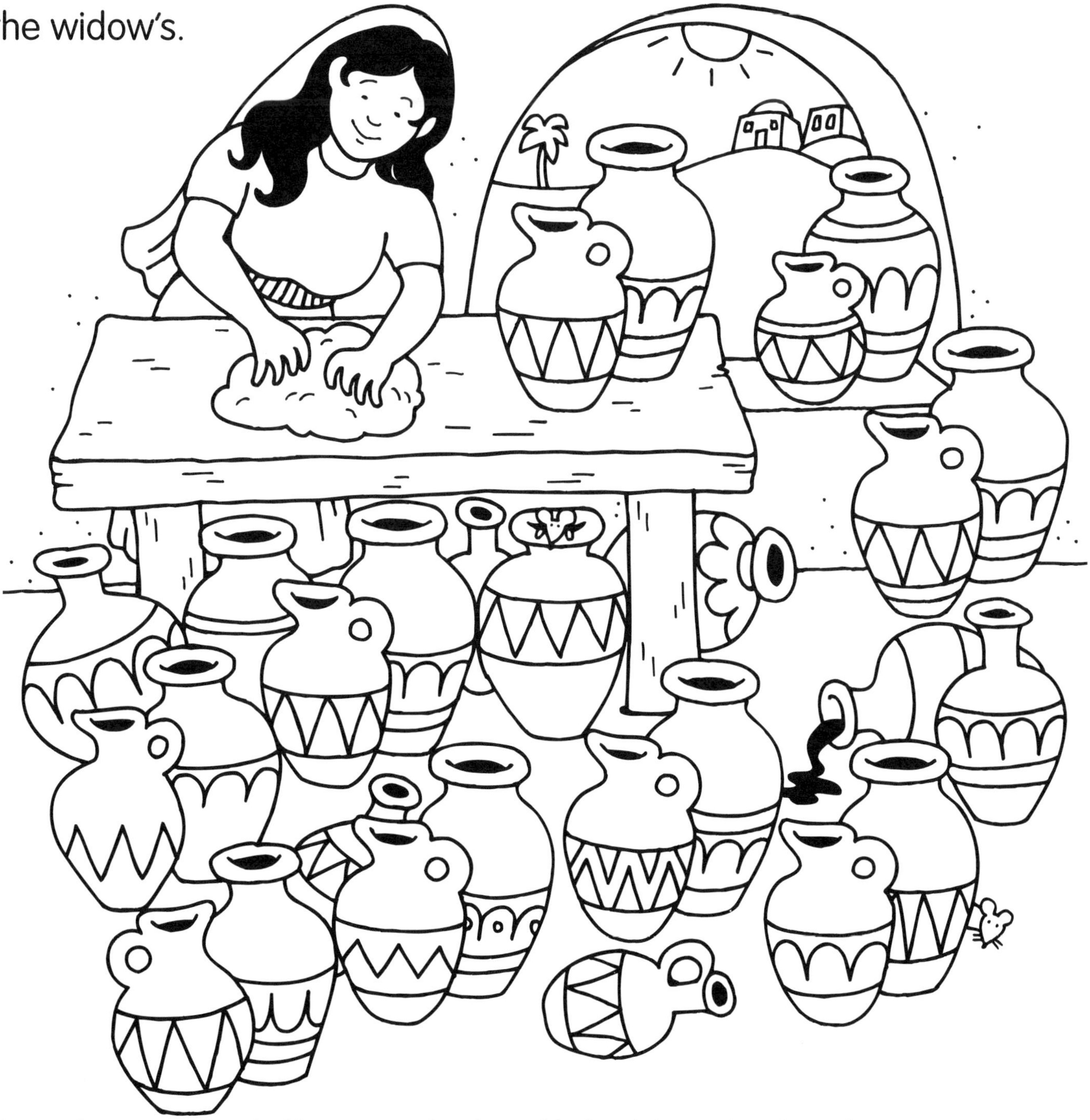

The widow was afraid of having no food. God helped the widow have food.
God helps us when we're afraid, too.
Our Bible tells us, "God said, 'Do not be afraid, for I am with you.'" (See Genesis 26:24.)

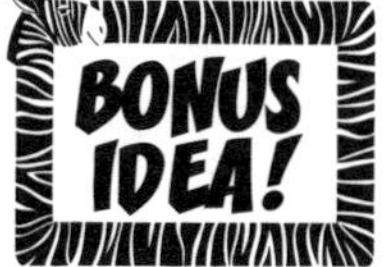

BONUS IDEA! On the blank lines write the beginning sound of each picture to find a great thing to remember:

God is ___ ___ ___ ___ ___ ___.

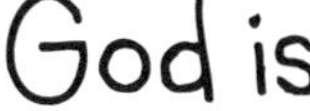

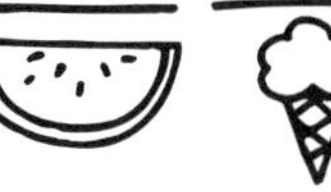

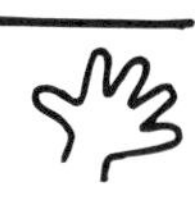

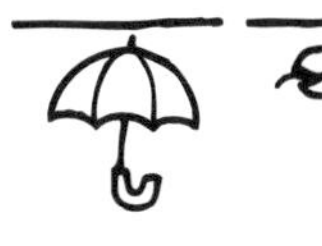

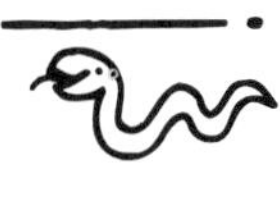

In each row, color the picture that is the same size as the picture in the box.

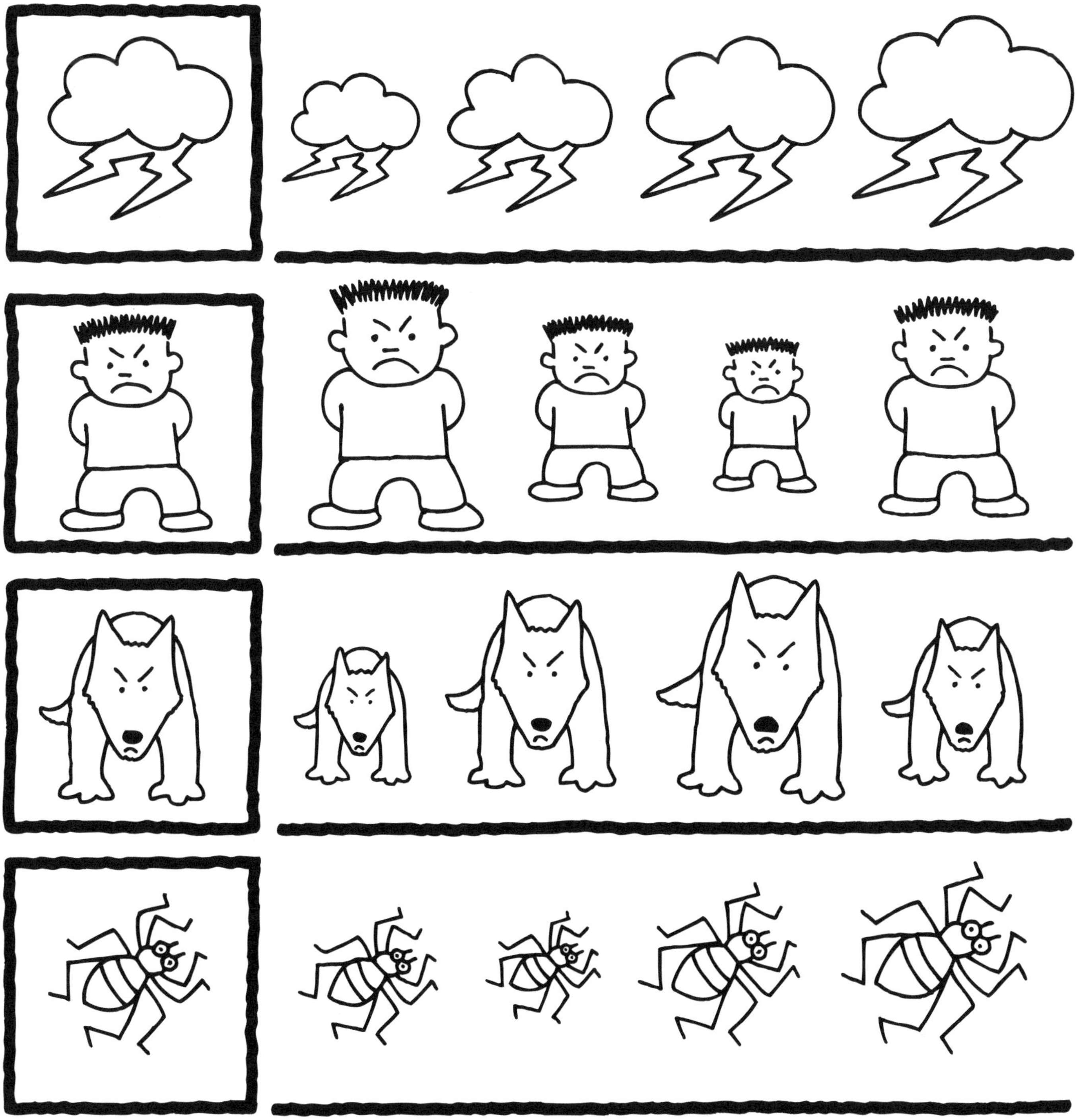

When we are afraid, we can remember God is with us.
Our Bible tells us, "God said, 'Do not be afraid, for I am with you.'" (See Genesis 26:24.)

Draw an ✖ on the pictures that might make you afraid.

Color in the spaces with numbers to see 4 things in Elisha's new room.

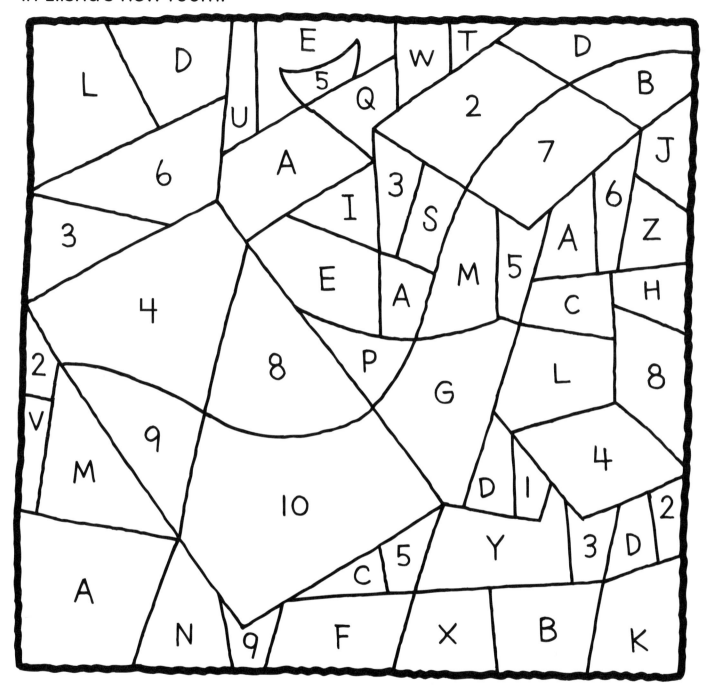

A kind woman and her husband made a room for Elisha.
God cared for Elisha.
God cares for us and gives us what we need.
Our Bible says, "God gives us what we need." (See Philippians 4:19.)

Draw a picture of 4 things in your room.
Thank God for giving you what you need!

In each row, draw an ✖ on the item that doesn't belong. Then, in the box, draw something that does belong.

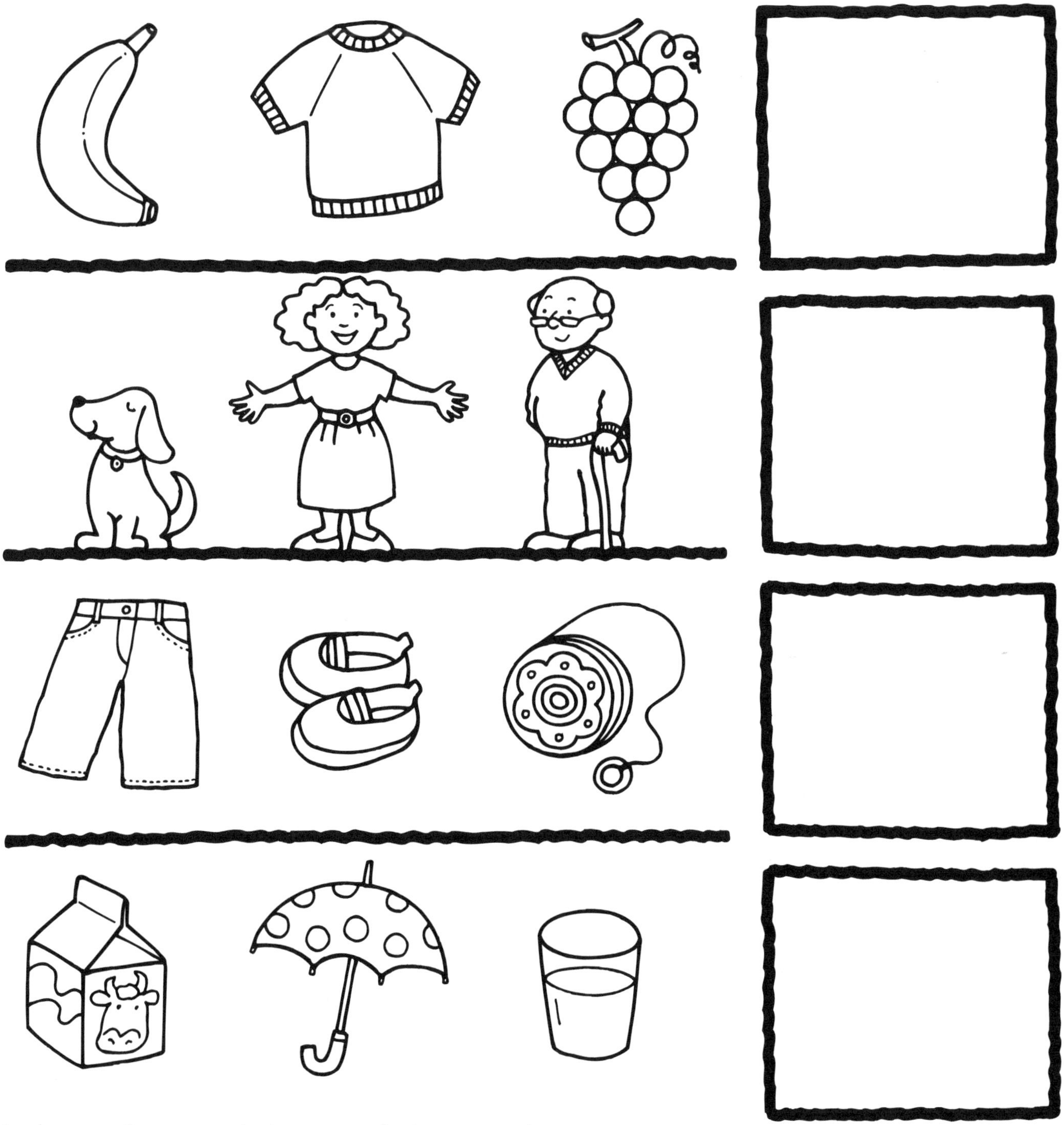

God cares for us and gives us what we need.
Our Bible says, "God gives us what we need." (See Philippians 4:19.)

Cut out the pictures you drew and glue them to a sheet of colored paper. Try to glue your drawings so that they are ordered from the smallest to the biggest.

Draw lines to match each shadow to its shape in the picture.

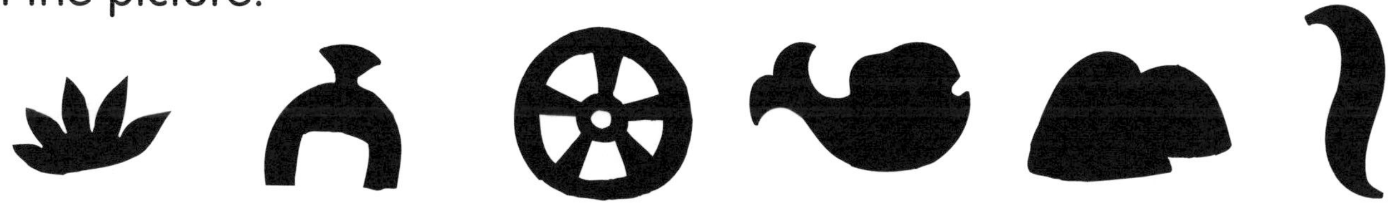

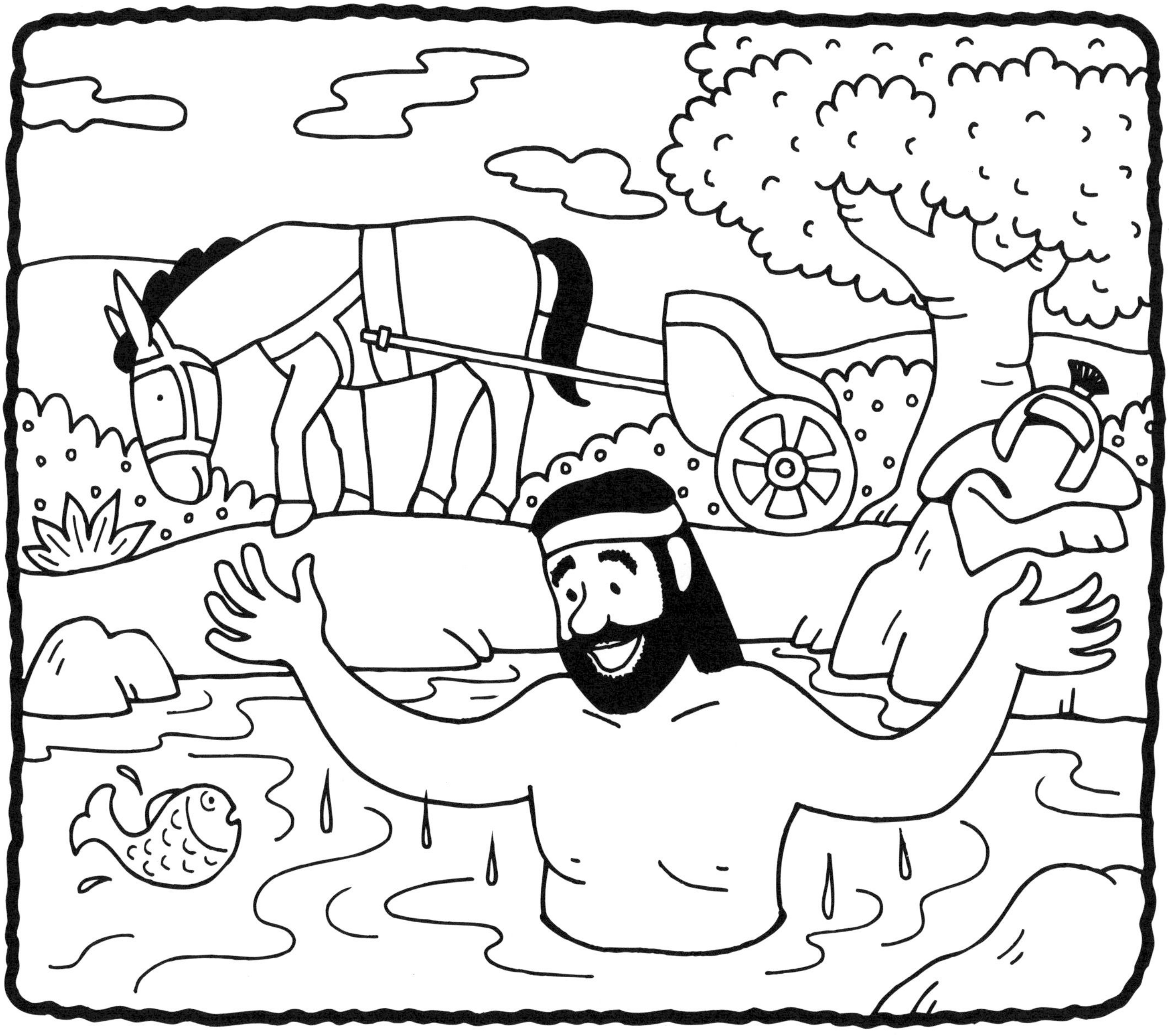

God showed His power by making Naaman well.
God is powerful and can help us, too!
Our Bible says, "Lord, you are great and powerful." (See Jeremiah 10:6.)

God showed His power when Naaman went into the river 7 times.
Say the word **powerful** 7 times as fast as you can.

Follow the maze to get to the ocean.

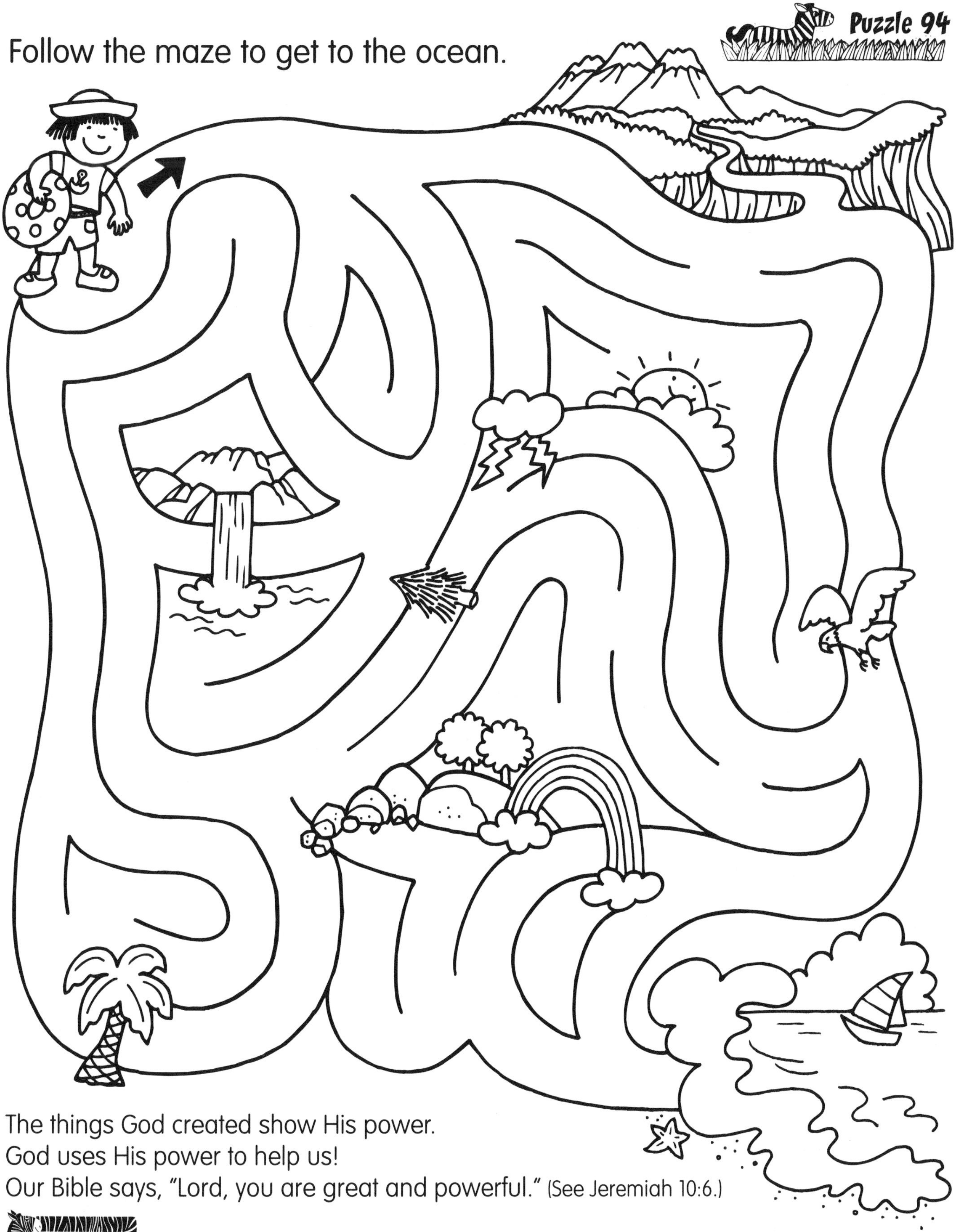

The things God created show His power.
God uses His power to help us!
Our Bible says, "Lord, you are great and powerful." (See Jeremiah 10:6.)

Draw a picture of a powerful thing God made.

Draw a ◯ around each object when you find it in the picture below.

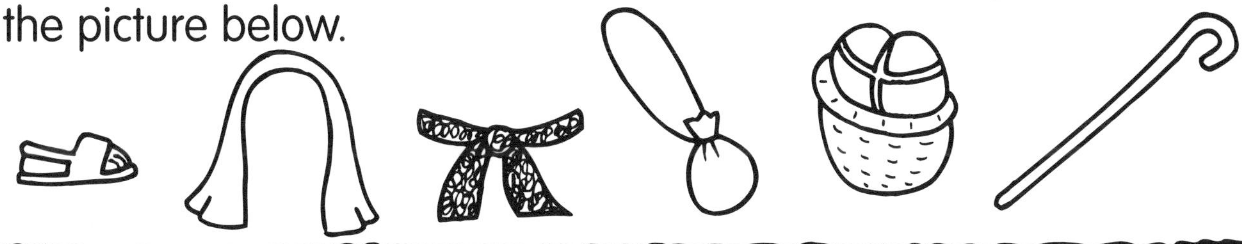

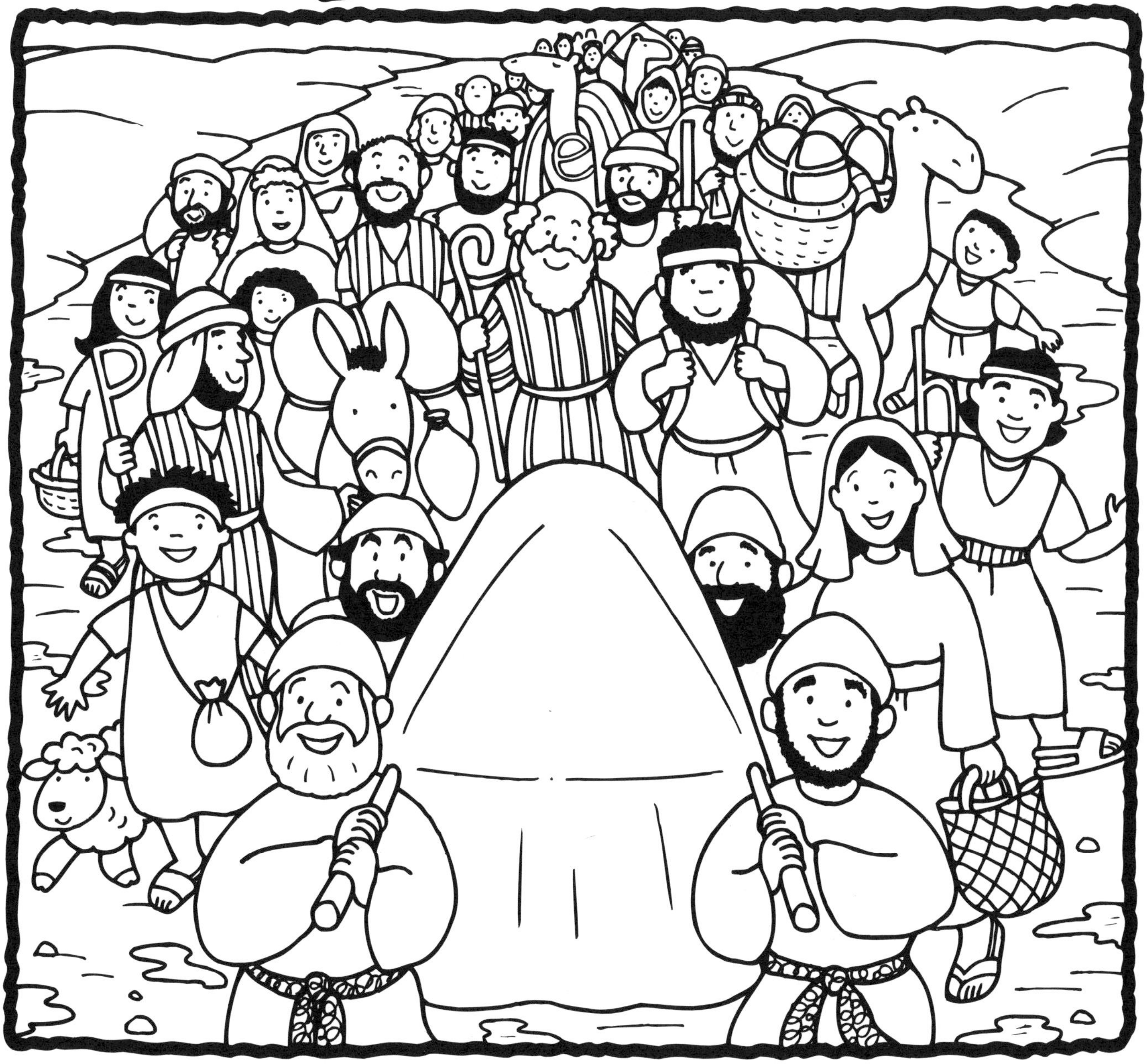

God helped the Israelites when they were crossing a big river.
God helps us, too.
Our Bible says, "The Lord is my helper; I will not be afraid." Hebrews 13:6

Trace these letters to remind you of what God does for you.
Then find these letters hidden in the picture above!

Copy the patterns to make the ladders exactly alike.

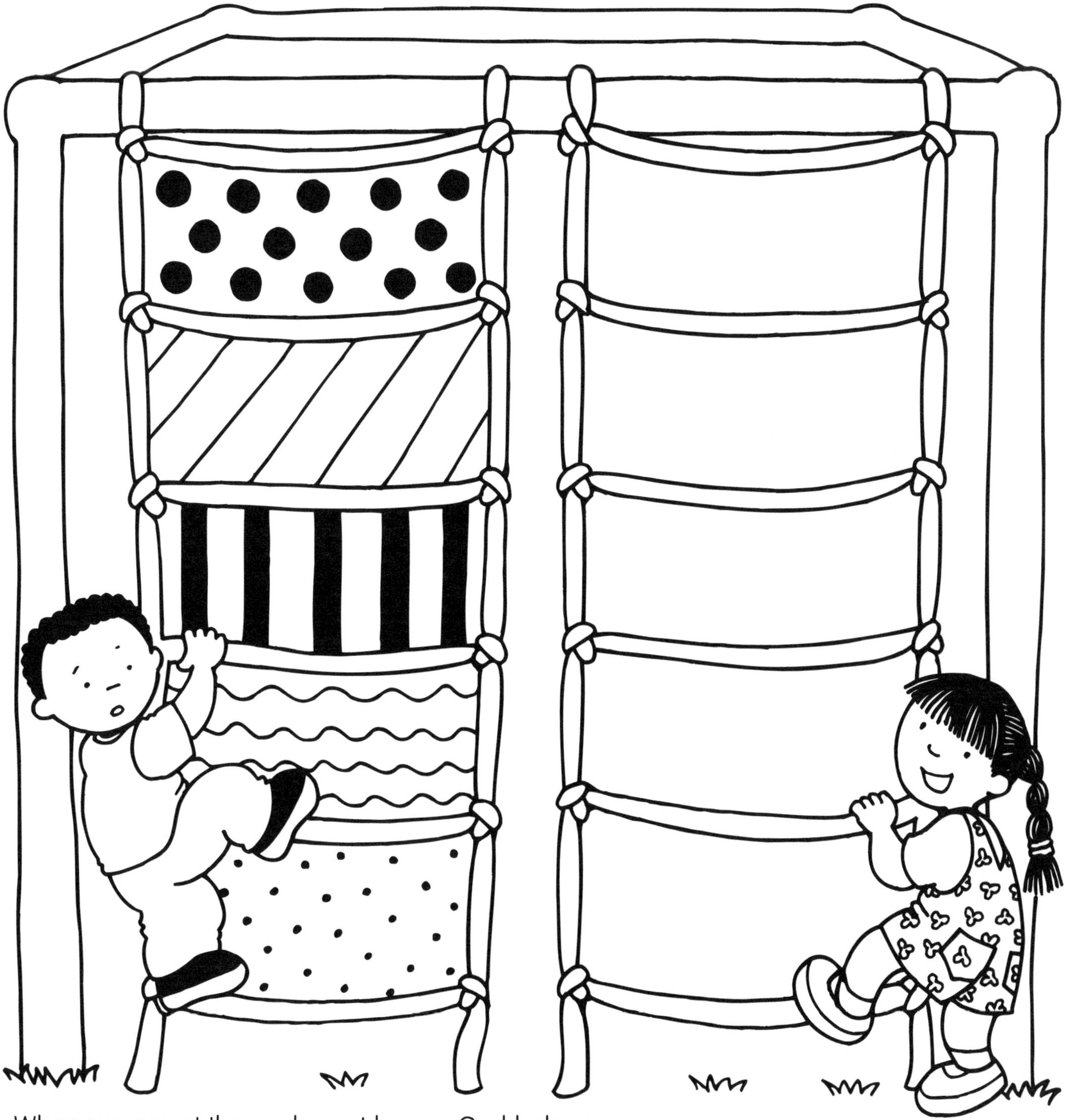

When we are at the park or at home, God helps us.
God helps us wherever we go.
Our Bible says, "The Lord is my helper; I will not be afraid." Hebrews 13:6

Draw a big △.
Draw lines across it to make 3 sections.
Draw a different pattern in each section.

Write the missing numbers in the □s.

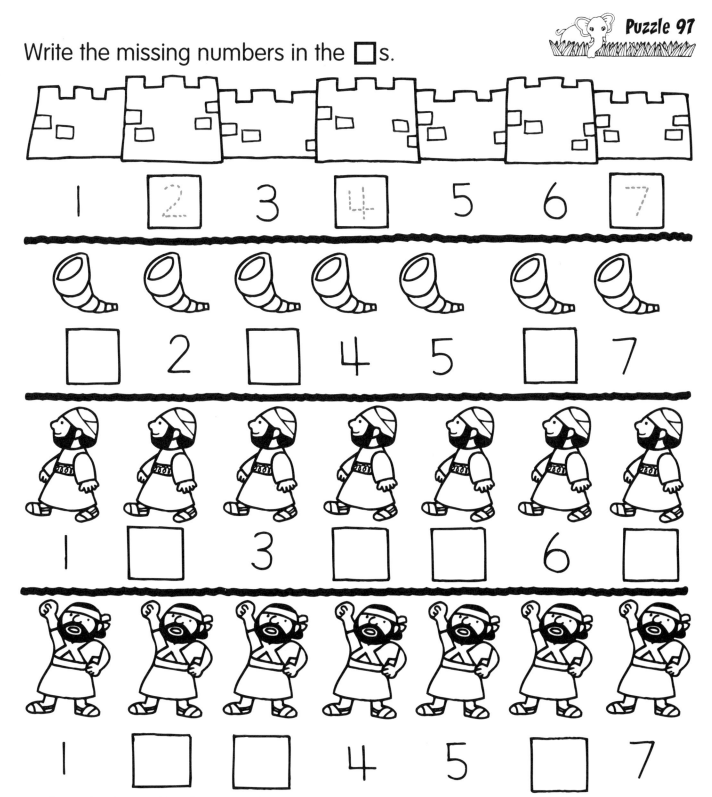

1 [2] 3 [4] 5 6 [7]

□ 2 □ 4 5 □ 7

1 □ 3 □ □ 6 □

1 □ □ 4 5 □ 7

God made the walls of Jericho fall down.
Joshua trusted in God.
Our Bible says, "I trust in the Lord." Psalm 31:6

Color 3  s YELLOW. Color 4  s GREEN. Color 5 s RED.

In each row, write numbers in the small boxes to put the pictures in order. Then cut out the pictures and glue them in order on a separate sheet of paper.

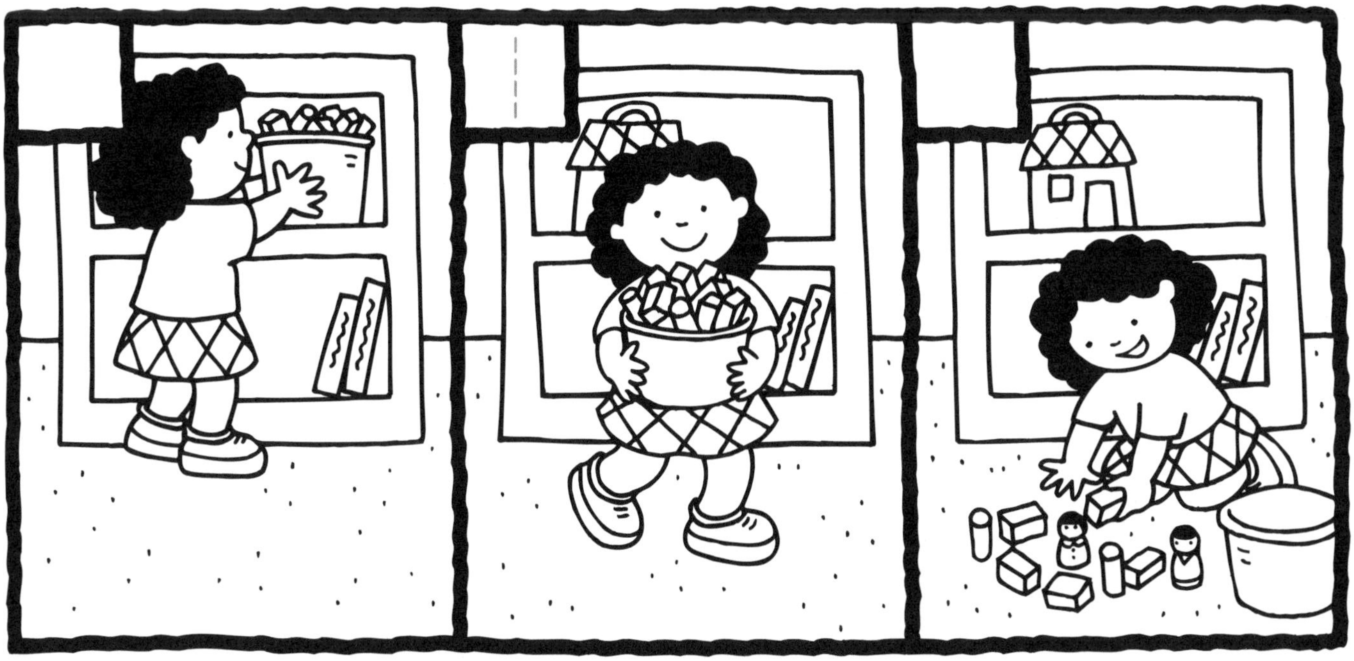

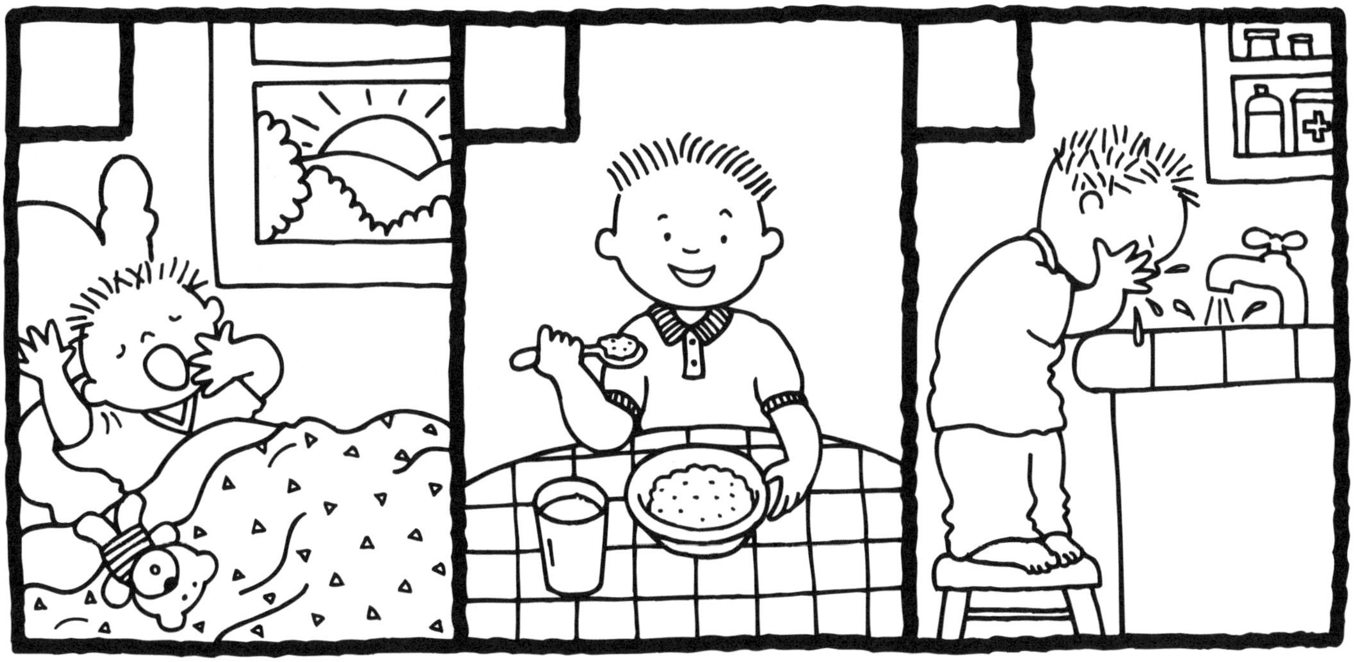

Which of these things do you do each day?
We can be sure that God will help us and love us every day.
Our Bible says, "I trust in the Lord." Psalm 31:6

BONUS IDEA! Draw a picture of something you do every day.

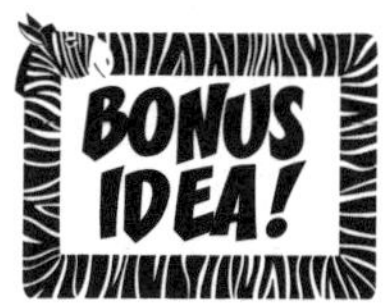

Draw a palm tree in the box by following the steps.

1. Draw

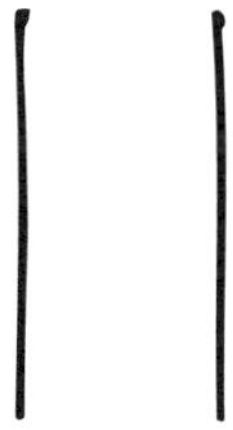

2. Add

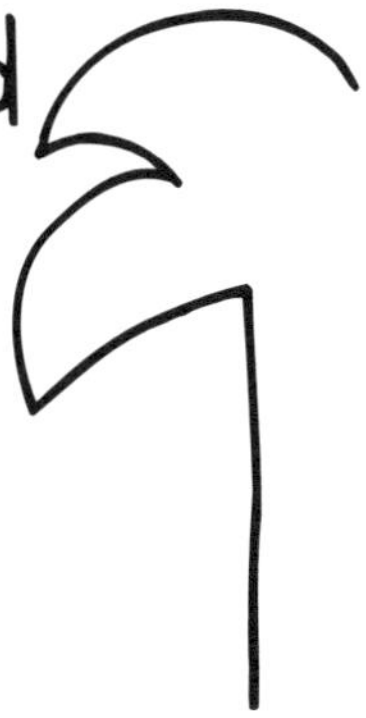

3. Add

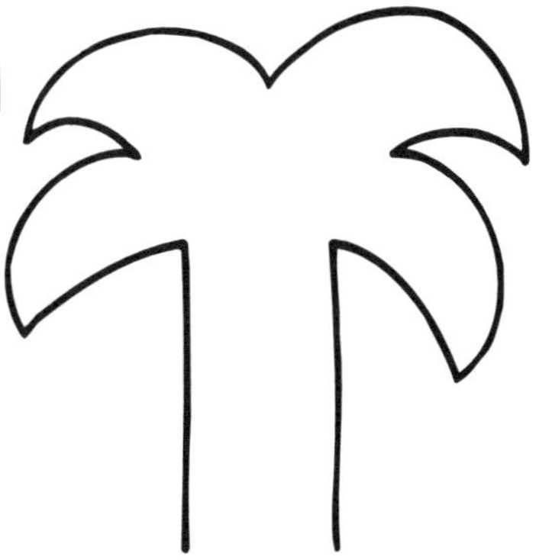

4. Add

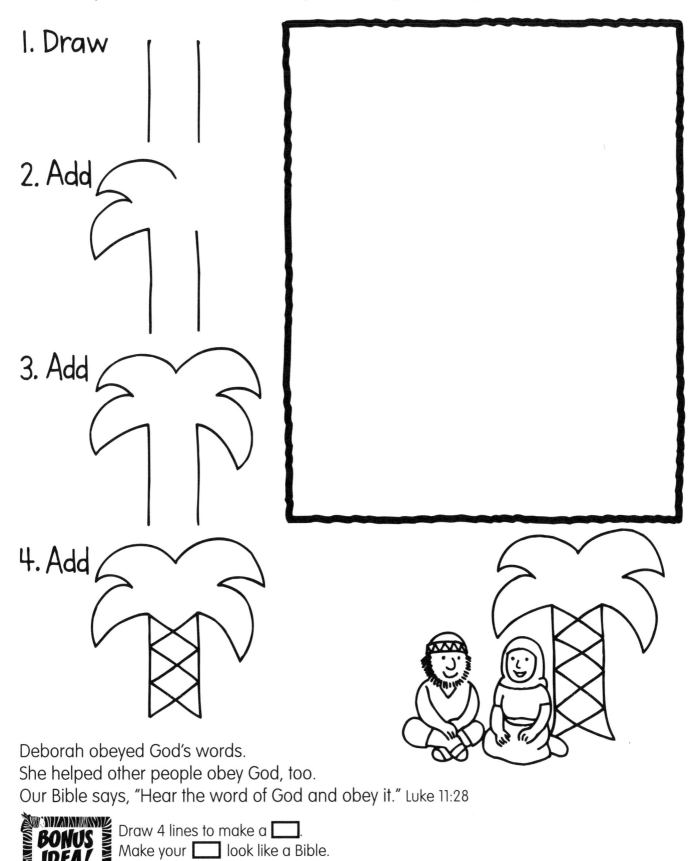

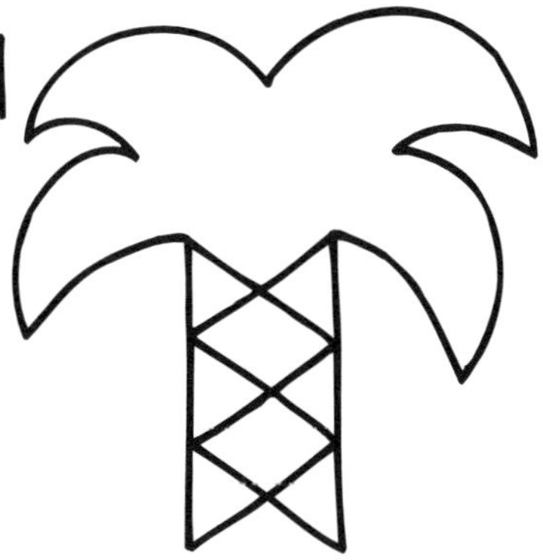

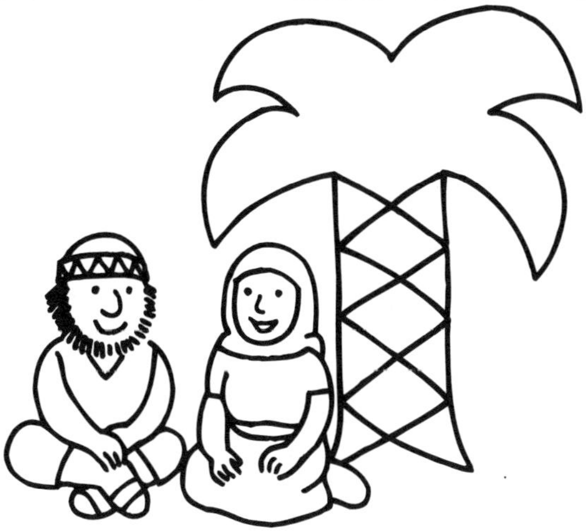

Deborah obeyed God's words.
She helped other people obey God, too.
Our Bible says, "Hear the word of God and obey it." Luke 11:28

Draw 4 lines to make a ▭.
Make your ▭ look like a Bible.
Tell someone 1 thing that God's Word, the Bible, says to do.

Color each girl YELLOW.
Color each boy BROWN.

Which person in this picture is obeying God's Word?
Find out by completing the dot-to-dot.

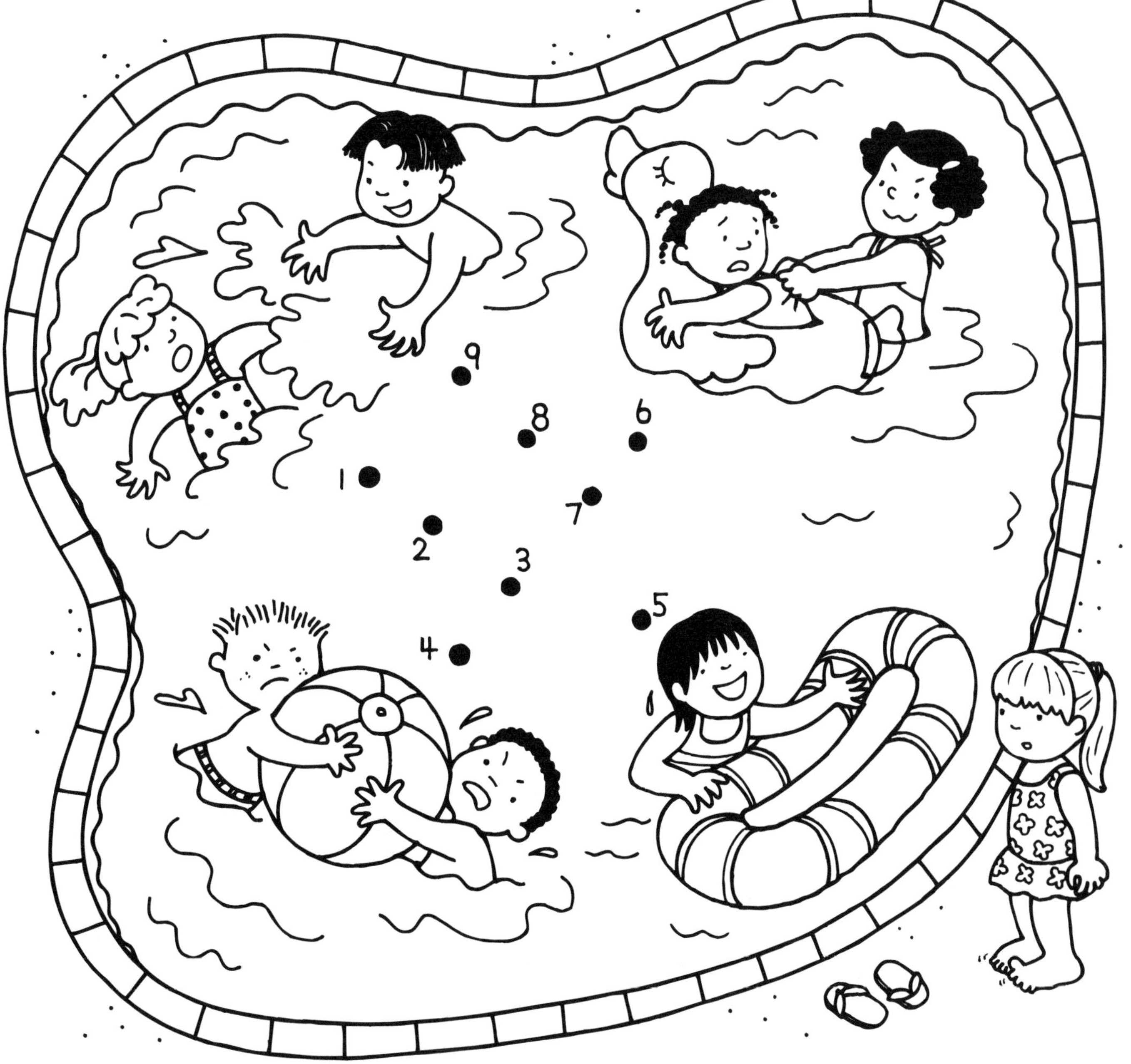

We can obey God's Word by doing what it says.
Our Bible says, "Hear the word of God and obey it." Luke 11:28

God's Word tells us to share with others.
Trace your hand on a sheet of paper.
Then draw something in your hand that you can share with someone.

Count each kind of object in the picture.
Write the correct number next to each object.

1 2 3 4 5 6 7 8

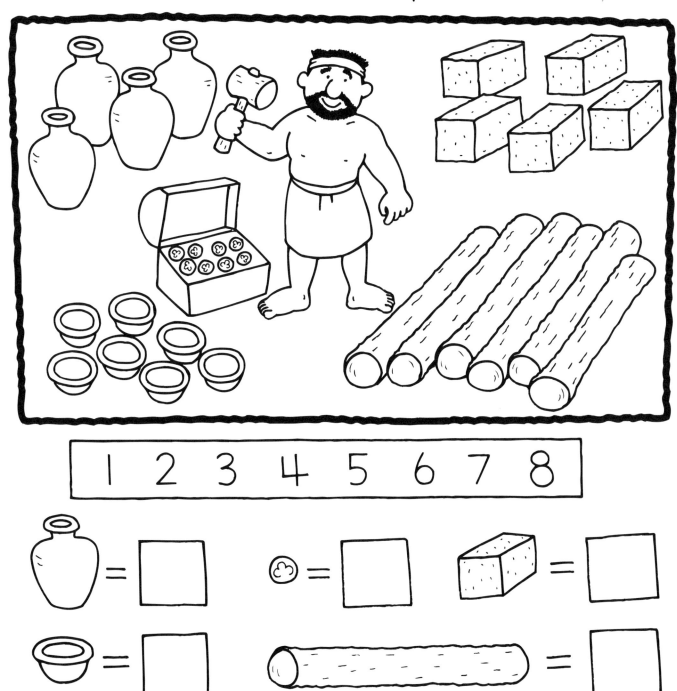

Joash helped God's people obey God by fixing the Temple.
We can learn from other people what God wants us to do, too.
Our Bible says, "Teach me your way, O Lord." Psalm 27:11

Write the beginning letter on each object.

These pictures show ways to learn from others.
In each row, draw a ◯ around the picture that shows **more** of something.

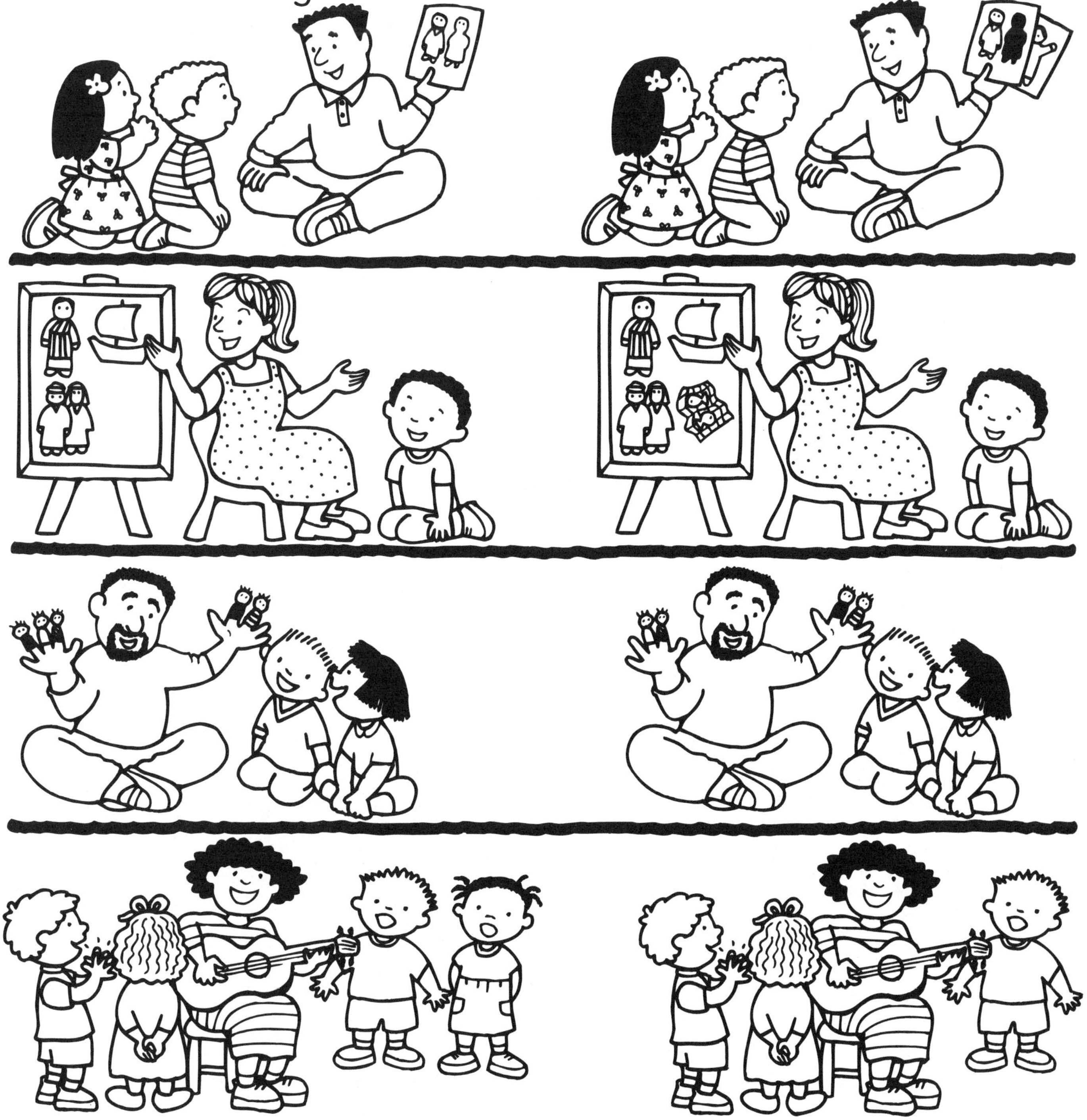

We can learn from other people about ways to obey God.
Our Bible says, "Teach me your way, O Lord." Psalm 27:11

Think of 1 person who teaches you about God.
Draw a thank-you picture for that person.

Draw a ◯ around the little pictures that are part of the big picture.
Draw an ✖ on the little pictures that are not part of the big picture.

Queen Esther did good by helping God's people stay safe.
God helps us be ready to do good.
Our Bible says, "Be ready to do whatever is good." Titus 3:1

Draw a ◯ around all the objects in the picture that start with a **G**.

Follow the footprints to see which child is obeying.

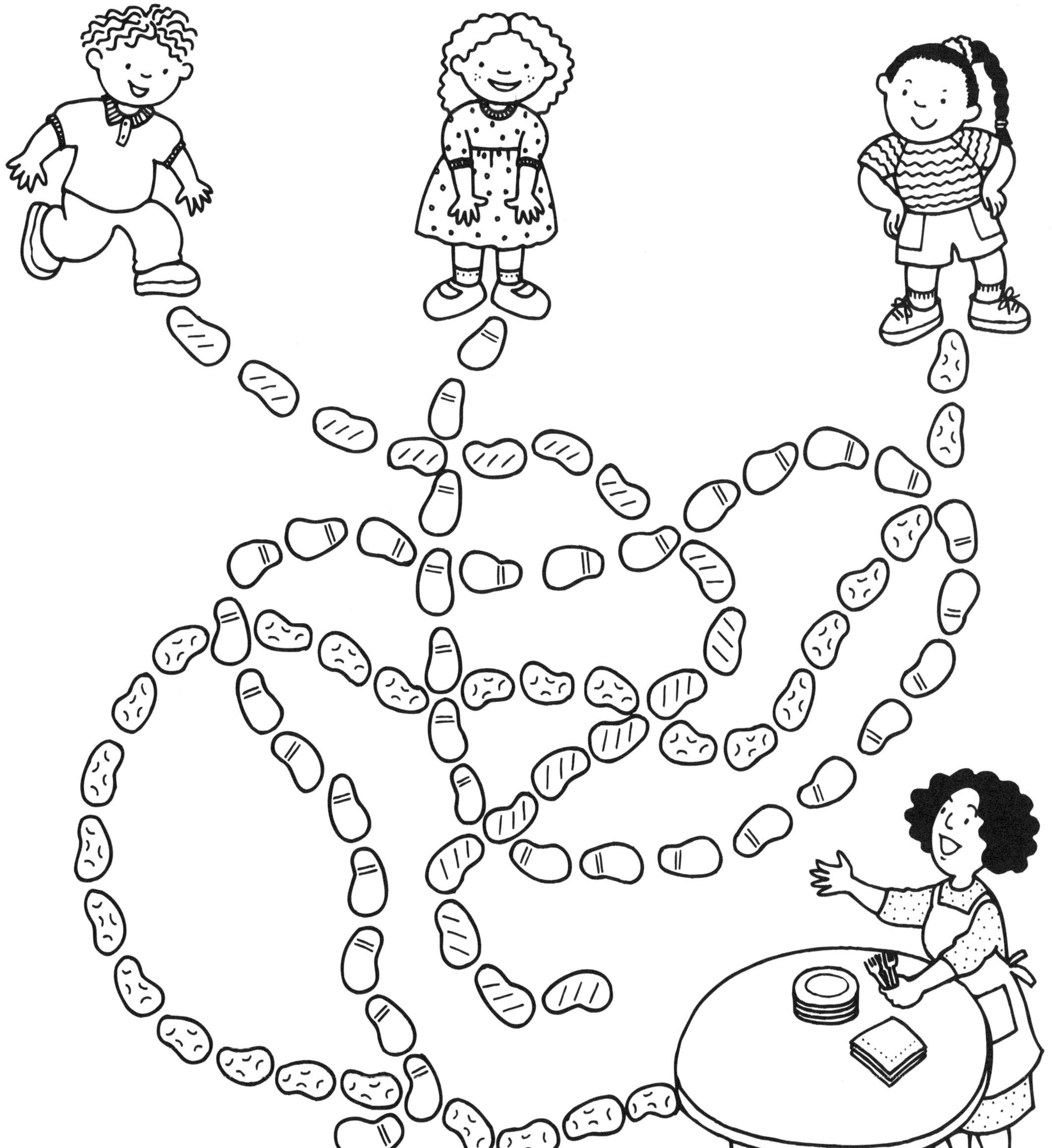

God helps us do good things.
Our Bible says, "Be ready to do whatever is good." Titus 3:1

Draw a picture to show a way you can use 1 of these objects to do good.

Bible Story Index *(in Bible order)*

OLD TESTAMENT

NEW TESTAMENT

Bible Verse Index *(in Bible order)*

Skills Index

ALPHABET
(Reading Readiness)

COLORS

DOT-TO-DOTS

HAND-EYE COORDINATION

LOGIC AND REASONING

MAZES

NUMBERS (Math Readiness)

OBSERVATION SKILLS

SHAPES

Topical Index

GOD'S LOVE AND CARE

JESUS' BIRTH

JESUS DIES AND LIVES AGAIN

JESUS LOVES AND TEACHES ME

LOVING GOD

OBEYING GOD AND DOING GOOD

SHOWING GOD'S LOVE TO OTHERS

TELLING OTHERS ABOUT JESUS

THANKING GOD